W9-AYK-910

BRAIN POWER

BRAIN POWER

**Maximize Communication and Cognition
for Your Business Success**

SHANNON BRADFORD

JOHN WILEY & SONS, INC.

8/02   INGRAM

Copyright © 2002 by Shannon Bradford. All rights reserved.

Published by John Wiley & Sons, Inc., New York.
Published simultaneously in Canada.

Modern Postcard daily e-mail update reprinted by permission of Modern Postcard.
©2001 by Modern Postcard® All Rights Reserved.

Excerpts from James O'Toole's list of GM's operating assumptions reprinted by permission of
John Wiley & Sons, Inc. from *Leading Change*, James O'Toole, ©1995 by Jossey-Bass Inc.,
Publishers.

Excerpts from PSS's Top 20 reprinted by permission of John Wiley & Sons, Inc. from *Faster
Company*, Patrick Kelly with John Case, ©1998 by Physician Sales and Service Inc. and John
Case.

"How Am I Doing?" report from Central Reservation Service reprinted by permission of Carlos
Giraldo, Central Reservation Service.

Post-it® is a registered trademark of 3M.

No part of this publication may be reproduced, stored in a retrieval system or transmitted in any
form or by any means, electronic, mechanical, photocopying, recording, scanning or otherwise,
except as permitted under Sections 107 or 108 of the 1976 United States Copyright Act, without
either the prior written permission of the Publisher, or authorization through payment of the
appropriate per-copy fee to the Copyright Clearance Center, 222 Rosewood Drive, Danvers, MA
01923, (978) 750-8400, fax (978) 750-4744. Requests to the Publisher for permission should be
addressed to the Permissions Department, John Wiley & Sons, Inc., 605 Third Avenue, New
York, NY 10158-0012, (212) 850-6011, fax (212) 850-6008, E-Mail: PERMREQ@WILEY.COM.

This publication is designed to provide accurate and authoritative information in regard to the
subject matter covered. It is sold with the understanding that the publisher is not engaged in
rendering legal, accounting, or other professional services. If legal advice or other expert
assistance is required, the services of a competent professional person should be sought.

Designations used by companies to distinguish their products are often claimed as trademarks.
In all instances where John Wiley & Sons, Inc. is aware of a claim, the product names appear in
initial capital or all capital letters. Readers, however, should contact the appropriate companies
for more complete information regarding trademarks and registration.

Library of Congress Cataloging-in-Publication Data:

Bradford, Shannon.
  Brain power : maximize communication and cognition for your
business success / by Shannon Bradford.
     p. cm.

  Includes bibliographical records and index.
  ISBN 0-471-20188-X (cloth : alk. paper)
    1. Business communication. I. Title: Maximize communication and
  cognition for your business success. II. Title.
HF5718 .B6914 2002
651.7—dc21   2002001015

Printed in the United States of America.

10 9 8 7 6 5 4 3 2 1

HF
5718
.B 6914
2002

CONTENTS

8   Brain Operating Principle 6: What You Focus On Expands   149
What people focus on will grow in their perception

9   Brain Operating Principle 7: What You Resist Persists   175
When people give their attention to something or
push against something by resisting it, that something
will persist

INTRODUCTION

This book began as a question. Why are some people and organizations thriving in today's new business world while others are struggling?

My burning curiosity about this question pushed me to start a research project. I read magazine articles and books. I talked to people in entrepreneurial start-ups and Fortune 100 companies. At the same time, I was working as a consultant and coach, observing the daily struggles and successes of people in companies large and small.

It wasn't until I read Kevin Kelly's landmark book in 1998, *New Rules for the New Economy: 10 Radical Strategies for a Connected World,* that my research and observations coalesced into one big idea. In his book, Kelly pointed out that one of the three distinguishing characteristics of the new economy is that it "favors intangible things—ideas, information, and relationships." (Kelly, K., 1998, p. 2) As I pondered this insight and thought about how the strange, new rules Kelly outlined could apply to my clients' businesses, the big idea struck me. The difference between success and failure in this new environment is *thinking.* I realized that the people and organizations on the leading edge were in that position because they were thinkers. Those who created profitable new products did so because they were thinkers. Those who took an innovative idea and made it successful did so because they were thinkers.

The impression created by stories in the media about the people and organizations on the leading edge was that in order to succeed in this new world, you had to be young, brainy, technical, and working in a start-up company. I wondered: Would there be the equivalent of a caste system in this new world? One that would separate those young, brainy, techies in start-ups from the rest of us? Or could the rest of us learn to operate our brains in a new way? Could we learn to change our thinking, to direct our brains, in order to succeed in this environment?

Looking at the characteristics of the new business environment, I decided there were four major groups of thinking skills that were critical to success. These four groups were:

I Changing the way you see and think about business.

I Generating ideas.

I Getting things done.

I Building good working relationships.

With those four groups in mind, I started paying close attention to what happened when people got stuck and when they excelled in those areas. I began to see some patterns.

It was identifying those patterns in real-life work situations, combined with learning about the latest research in brain science, surveying psychological theory, and reading business books and magazines, that sparked the idea of the Original Search Engine brain and the seven Brain Operating Principles.

As I identified the principles, I tried them out (along with the action tools) with my clients and in training seminars; in response, people immediately raved about what a difference it made for them to understand the workings of their brains and to feel that they were in the driver's seat, instead of being at the mercy of a runaway brain. So, I began to focus on teaching people the thinking skills they needed to think differently, generate ideas, get things done, and build great working relationships.

This book, *Brain Power*, reveals the dynamics of how people think and how you can use the seven Brain Operating Principles to think, learn, and communicate more successfully in business.

I wrote this book to help individuals and organizations survive and thrive in this new business environment. Whether you are a knowledge worker, an entrepreneur, a manager, or a CEO, you will benefit from the concepts and skills you learn.

Brain Power is based on my belief that people can learn to direct their brains, can learn emotional intelligence, can learn to communicate more effectively, and can learn creativity. In this book, I'll tell you *how*.

More specifically, in *Brain Power*, you'll learn how to:

I Direct your brain to solve problems and generate ideas.

I Identify and discard old assumptions that block innovation and new ideas.

I Improve relationships with other people, including employees, colleagues, and customers.

I Ease stress and tension.

I Strengthen internal communication in companies.

I Improve employee retention.

I Persuade customers and colleagues.

I Break through and prevent procrastination.

I Manage change and transitions.

I Work more effectively in teams.

I Enhance customer satisfaction.

I Understand conflicts between generations.

You'll also learn from stories about people who have used the principles:

I How learning about Mental Maps and articulating expectations made a significant difference in the working relationships *and* the financial results of a technology company.

I How a focus on exploring showed a business owner a new opportunity.

I How a business woman used repetition to learn to ask for what she needed.

I How a company learned to combat e-expectations by telling customers what to expect.

I How two entrepreneurs overcame paralysis by snipping a perfectionist loop.

I How learning about maps turned two feuding colleagues into
teammates.

I How using visualization helped a client overcome the anxiety of
an unfamiliar challenge.

I How giving in helped a job hunter who was resisting rejection.

Brain Power includes nine chapters.

NOT YOUR FATHER'S ECONOMY: WHAT HAS CHANGED AND WHY THINKING = VALUE

The dynamics of today's economy are very different from the old, industrial economy. The shift from tangibles to intangibles means that
the ability to think is a critical success factor in today's world. In this
chapter, you'll learn the key characteristics of this economy, why
thinking is so valuable in this new environment, and how individuals
and organizations can nurture thinking.

THE ORIGINAL SEARCH ENGINE BRAIN

How can people and organizations learn to think more effectively if
they don't know *how* they think in the first place? In this chapter,
you'll learn why the brain is the Original Search Engine, the physiology of how your brain makes thinking connections, and a few key psychological theories that form the foundation for the Brain Operating
Principles.

BRAIN OPERATING PRINCIPLE 1: BERMUDA TRIANGLES OF INFORMATION

*Given a black hole of information, people will fill the hole with negative
conclusions.*

When there is uncertainty or a lack of communication in the workplace, people tend to assume the negative. Learn how these negative assumptions affect employees and customers, the role of feedback and information in preventing black holes, the dynamic of e-expectations, and how you can motivate and retain employees and satisfy customers by preventing Bermuda Triangles.

ACTION TOOLS

▌ The 5:1 Feedback Ratio.
▌ External Bermuda Triangles Scan.

BRAIN OPERATING PRINCIPLE 2: DRIVE FOR CLOSURE

People strive for completion or a definitive answer even when neither exists.

The urge to have completion or a definitive answer is a particular problem in today's ambiguous, paradoxical business environment. The Drive for Closure causes problems in working relationships, it shuts down innovation, and it pushes people to make bad decisions. Learn to use your Drive for Closure, instead, to generate ideas, to break through procrastination, and to persuade.

ACTION TOOL

▌ The 15-Minute Bribe.

BRAIN OPERATING PRINCIPLE 3: INFINITE LOOP THINKING

When people are stuck in a thinking loop, they are unable to see alternatives.

Individuals and organizations get stuck in thinking loops that blind them to possibilities and alternatives. Learn how to identify worry loops, infinitely right loops, perfection loops, groupthink and process loops, and discover how to lower stress and avert disaster by snipping those loops.

ACTION TOOLS

I Get Off the Merry-Go-Round.

I The Circular Box.

BRAIN OPERATING PRINCIPLE 4: MENTAL MAPS

People rely on Mental Maps, made up of assumptions and unwritten rules, as mental shortcuts.

Mental Maps are the equivalent of prescription eyeglasses; they influence how individuals and organizations perceive the world. Learn how Mental Maps impact working relationships, strategy, customers, and the ability of an organization to innovate and change. Find out how to identify assumptions and unwritten rules and the importance of learning how to change your maps.

ACTION TOOLS

I Take Me to Your Leader.

I Telling Stories.

BRAIN OPERATING PRINCIPLE 5: REPETITION REQUIRED

People need repetition to learn, whether it is a new skill, instructions for a task, or meeting business goals.

You grew up hearing the phrase, practice makes perfect. What you probably didn't know is that when you learn something new, your brain is actually building physical connections. Find out how to use repetition to learn new skills, communicate business goals, and condition yourself and your organization for success.

ACTION TOOL

▮ Theme Song.

BRAIN OPERATING PRINCIPLE 6: WHAT YOU FOCUS ON EXPANDS

What people focus on will grow in their perception.

The questions you ask and what you choose to focus on will determine your experience of the world. Learn how the principle of What You Focus On Expands affects goal-setting, working relationships, an organization's ability to execute, and customer satisfaction. Identify your focus and learn how to shift when you're focused on the wrong things.

ACTION TOOLS

▮ The Ritual Shift.
▮ Corporate Myopia.

BRAIN OPERATING PRINCIPLE 7: WHAT YOU RESIST PERSISTS

When people give their attention to something or push against something by resisting it, that something will persist.

When individuals and organizations resist, they strengthen what they are resisting. Learn how resisting something can cause it to happen, how resistant denial and procrastination affect individuals and or-

ganizations, as well as the consequences of resisting change. Then discover the paradoxical benefits of giving in.

ACTION TOOL

❚ The Yield Sign.

HOW TO USE THIS BOOK

There are two ways to use this book. One is to read through the chapters from start to finish. Another is to use the Brain Operating Principles Symptoms Quiz or the Brain Operating Principles Solutions Quiz to identify which principles you or your organization may be struggling with or which principles would be helpful to use. Each of the chapters on a Brain Operating Principle describes how the principle applies to both individuals and organizations, and each includes anecdotes about the effect of the principle on people and organizations (NOTE: In sharing anecdotes about clients, their names have been changed to protect their privacy). Each chapter also includes a list of key points, as well as action tools for using the principles in your job.

The action tools are at-work strategies that you can use to apply the Brain Operating Principles to your working life. They provide suggestions for how the principles might be operating in your brain, your job, or your organization. The action tools also supply strategies for making the principles work for you. Some of the action tools are short, simple strategies. Other tools take a little more time and effort to implement. There are a few action tools that you will find to be more effective if you involve other people from your organization when you use them.

It is important to recognize that the principles don't necessarily operate independently of each other. For example, an individual or organization could have Drive for Closure, Infinite Loop Thinking, and What You Focus On Expands all operating at the same time and causing problems. Also, when used as solutions, the principles may need to be used in combination. For example, an organization that is going through a major change needs to pay special attention to Bermuda Triangles, Repetition Required, Mental Maps, and What You Resist Persists.

THE BRAIN OPERATING PRINCIPLES SYMPTOMS QUIZ

The symptoms quiz helps you identify which Brain Operating Principles are operating in your brain (or in your organization's collective brain). Once you've identified the principles, you can learn about how the principles operate, and use the action tools to put yourself (or your organization) in the driver's seat.

Instructions: If you, or your organization, are experiencing one of these symptoms, check the box next to the symptom.

1. There are lots of rumors circulating in your organization. ☐
2. You (or your organization) are stuck in same thinking about a problem or situation. ☐
3. You are sabotaging yourself. ☐
4. There is conflict between generations in your organization. ☐
5. Your organization has a branch office that feels like it's a second-class citizen. ☐
6. Critics are heroes in your organization. ☐
7. You are procrastinating about working on a project. ☐
8. People in your organization complain they never know what is going on. ☐
9. Your organization is clinging to core competencies in the face of change. ☐
10. You are stuck in a worry loop. ☐
11. Your organization is struggling with a major industry change. ☐
12. There is a lot of internal competition in your organization. ☐
13. Your organization is searching for a silver bullet solution. ☐
14. You have a particular type of recurring conflict. ☐
15. Your customers (internal or external) have unrealistic expectations about production times. ☐
16. You feel stuck in a negative focus. ☐

17. You feel compelled to make a decision now, even though you know you should wait. ☐

18. In your organization, there is too much energy invested in process, not enough in results. ☐

19. Your organization needs to change its business assumptions. ☐

20. Your organization suffers from never-ending reorganization. ☐

21. You are struggling to learn a new skill. ☐

22. There is an overemphasis on control in your organization. ☐

23. In your organization, there is too much emphasis on numbers. ☐

24. Your organization is trying to communicate about a major change. ☐

25. You are stuck because of perfectionist thinking. ☐

26. You are feeling very anxious about an unfamiliar situation. ☐

27. You are having a major conflict with someone in your organization. ☐

28. When you arrive at the office, you feel anxiety or dread, but you don't know why. ☐

Now circle the numbers below that correspond to the symptoms you checked above.

Bermuda Triangles of Information	1	5	15	26
Drive for Closure	7	13	17	22
Infinite Loop Thinking	2	10	18	25
Mental Maps	4	11	19	27
Repetition Required	8	21	24	28
What You Focus On Expands	6	12	16	23
What You Resist Persists	3	9	14	20

Your circles identify which principles you (or your organization) need to learn. (If you circled them all or circled a majority of the principles, don't worry, you're not alone.)

THE BRAIN OPERATING PRINCIPLES SOLUTIONS QUIZ

The solutions quiz helps you identify which Brain Operating Principles could help you (or your organization) in your upcoming initiatives.

Instructions: If you or your organization need to accomplish one of the goals below, check the box next to the goal.

1. Guide the organization through a period of uncertainty. ☐
2. Blend two organizations. ☐
3. Motivate and retain employees using feedback. ☐
4. Handle a trend. ☐
5. Build the confidence of employees to tackle a change. ☐
6. Build good working relationships among diverse groups. ☐
7. Persuade your colleagues to support a new project. ☐
8. Help employees through resistance to change. ☐
9. Overcome a history of arrogance. ☐
10. Reach a goal. ☐
11. Understand your customers better. ☐
12. Close a deal with a customer. ☐
13. Communicate change. ☐
14. Use communication to delight customers. ☐
15. Change careers. ☐
16. Work more effectively in a team. ☐
17. Improve relationships with customers. ☐
18. Generate ideas or solve problems. ☐

Now circle the numbers below that correspond to the goals you checked above.

Bermuda Triangles of Information	3	13	14	17
Drive for Closure	7	10	12	18
Infinite Loop Thinking	9	17		
Mental Maps	2	6	11	16
Repetition Required	1	13	14	
What You Focus On Expands	5	15	18	
What You Resist Persists	4	8		

Your circles identify which principles will help you or your organization accomplish your goals.

BRAIN
POWER

1

NOT YOUR FATHER'S ECONOMY: What Has Changed and Why Thinking = Value

What do you call the economy we're working in today? The Knowledge Economy? The Information Age? The Network Economy? The Attention Economy? The Intangibles Economy? The Digital Age? The Customer Economy? Whatever you call it, one thing is for sure—this is definitely not your father's economy.

It is easy to identify what this economy is not, but it is not easy to identify exactly what it is. Perhaps this is because we're living two business realities simultaneously. We look to the left and the landscape strongly resembles the old world. We look to the right and it's a brave new world. For people on the inside looking out in some large organizations, the world has barely changed. When they arrive at work each day, their jobs look the same as they did six months, one year, or even five years ago. They may read stories about the changed workplace, but that's not what they experience.

This economic schizophrenia may be why there are so many descriptive labels floating around and the only adjective that has stuck so far is *new* as in the *new economy*. This new economy is difficult to name because it is still evolving. Although there are some identifiable characteristics that differentiate it from previous economies, there isn't yet one descriptor that captures this economy so vividly that people agree on it and use it.

TAYLOR-INFLUENCED MANAGEMENT

The rules of business in the old days were based on the ideas we learned from Frederick Winslow Taylor—what I call Taylor-influenced

1

management. Frederick Taylor was an engineer who created the theory of Scientific Management in the early 1900s. As part of the theory, Taylor introduced the idea of time-and-motion studies to business. He would break a task into pieces and time each piece with a stopwatch. Then he would reassemble the job, based on the most efficient way to perform the task. Taylor had a big influence on mass production practices and on the business world in general.

With Scientific Management as a frame of reference, most organizations were built for:

I Certainty, predictability, routine.

I Hierarchy, control.

I Fear-based management.

I Five-year plans.

I Efficiency (the most output for least input).

I Acquiring and leveraging physical assets.

I People as factors of production.

I One best way, either-or.

I Build a better mousetrap.

I React to change.

These characteristics, the underpinnings of Taylor-influenced management, dominated the business world throughout most of the twentieth century. Organizations developed rules, procedures, strategies, and plans based on that viewpoint.

For example, ask anyone who graduated with a business degree what the primary functions of a manager are, and they will rattle off some version of the following: planning, organizing, staffing, supervising, and controlling. Even today, in an uncertain, nonlinear business world, would-be managers are taught that planning and controlling are their primary responsibilities.

Another example is the concept managers learned from Scientific Management that any variation in a task was a bad thing. Because of that idea, good managers shut down any variation by dictating policies, and by creating processes and routines. In *How Digital Is Your Business*, Adrian Slywotsky and David Morrison describe this viewpoint: "In a traditional nondigital business, the need to reduce the 'human factor' is very real. It's caused by the fact that many employees are engaged in low-value work—taking orders, filling out forms, transmitting data, tracking procedures, responding to routine requests for the thousandth time, and so on. Under such circumstances, the best thing a worker can do is behave like a reliable machine. Any other action can only delay or derail the process." (Slywotsky and Morrison, 2000, p. 280)

Even schools taught the Taylor-influenced mentality. They educated children by rewarding behaviors that would make them successful in a Taylorized world: punctuality, obedience, not questioning authority, tolerating repetition, and no expectation of enjoyment on the job.

THE NEW ENVIRONMENT

It's not that Taylor-influenced management was wrong. It worked very well for the businesses of the old, industrial economy, when the majority of tasks were repetitive, routine, and easily broken into discrete steps. It worked when the business world was predictable, logical, and linear. It worked when thinking was not a required skill for success.

However, the business environment that meshed with Taylor's theory is quickly dissolving and being replaced by a very different world. In this new world:

Customers Have More Choices and More Power

Today, customers have the ability to choose from a greater variety of competing suppliers. Technology gives customers access to more products and more companies. For example, instead of choosing only from large, well-known suppliers, customers can do business with smaller, lesser-known businesses. Instead of having to select a supplier from among a few suppliers in town, customers can buy from companies in another part of the country or even in a different part of the world. In addition to providing more choices, technology also gives customers greater power by making more information about products and companies available. With more information at their fingertips, customers can make better decisions about which products or companies best suit their needs.

With more choices and more power in the hands of customers, service and relationships take on an even greater importance for the long-term success of a company. Jack Welch, former CEO of GE, said of the impact of technology: "It will change relationships with customers. . . . Nothing will be hidden in paperwork. . . . Execution is very important. Every error you make is transparent on the Web." (Slywotsky and Morrison, 2000, p. 199)

Part of the new customer service is the ability to meet the demands of customers by providing a range of products and services, and making them available when customers want them. Customers expect to buy what they want, when they want it. These expectations created the new concept of businesses that run 24/7.

Intangibles Play a Larger Role

In the old days, most companies produced *stuff*, tangible products you could hold in your hands. Today, more and more businesses sell intangibles. With an intangible you can only hold a representation of the product in your hands; the essence of the product is invisible.

In *New Rules for the New Economy*, Kevin Kelly described the economic weight of intangibles: "The new economy deals in wispy entities such as information, relationships, copyright, entertainment, securities, and derivatives. The U.S. economy is already demassifying, drifting toward these intangibles. The creations most in demand from the United States (those exported) lost 50% of their physical weight per dollar of value in only six years." (Kelly, K., 1998, p. 3)

It's not just end products that are drifting toward intangibles. Even inputs are becoming less tangible. In a 1998 article in *Fortune* magazine, Thomas Stewart noted: "Overall, U.S. companies today need 20% less in tangible assets to produce a dollar's worth of sales than they did a quarter-century ago." (Stewart, 1998, p. 170) Stewart cited Lowell Bryan, a McKinsey partner, as his source for the statistic.

Intangibles require different processes of development, production, and marketing. Intangibles also require more knowledge work than tangible products, which explains why knowledge work is now a larger part of the business world.

The Keyword Is Uncertainty

George Conrades, CEO of Akamai, said during an interview with *Harvard Business Review*, "Our long term is 90 days. That's it. That's the longest forecast we ever make." (Carr, 2000, p. 122) Such comments illustrate the rapid change and uncertainty that are characteristic of today's business environment.

In an environment marked by change, uncertainty, paradox, and ambiguity, the old ideas about planning and controlling just don't work. Plans and controls were possible in the old, industrial economy, when the world was more predictable. In that environment, five-year plans were the norm, and companies could plan for the future based on the past. In fact, long-term forecasting—the process of setting goals for five to ten years into the future based on past performance—was an essential part of the planning process. But today, operating in the throes of a major shift, few companies can plan for the future based on the past. In a nonlinear environment, the future is not just more of the past.

Organizations Are Changing Shape

The way that people work in organizations and the way that organizations are structured have already changed far more than most people recognize. Both will continue to change as the business environment continues to evolve.

In today's business world, more people manipulate information and knowledge than parts and machinery. More work is accomplished in collaborative teamwork than on structured assembly lines. People are working in more diverse groups. Technology allows knowledge workers to function anywhere, anytime.

It is these factors, and others like them, that are changing the structure of organizations. In the old economy, organizations were structured in hierarchies and departments, and management emphasized getting the structure right because structure provided a measure of certainty. In addition, organizational charts and departmental silos meant that people could be certain who was in charge of which projects. They also provided guidance about the right people to talk to about issues and information.

Today, organizations are being structured as networks rather than hierarchies. Although departments still exist, they are more flexible and porous than the silos of the past. Working relationships and the ability to make things happen are emphasized over identifying the one right structure.

Another big change in the structure of organizations is size. It used to be that there were big businesses and there were Mom-&-Pop shops. Then along came a boom in small business. In a 1999 article in *Wired* magazine, Kevin Kelly put the issue of size into startling perspective: "Today there are 20 million enterprises and 130 million workers in the US; that means there is one company for every six and a half workers. Starting a business is becoming as routine as getting a job. In another 20 years, there could be 40 million enterprises, or one company for every three bodies in the workplace." (Kelly, K., 1999, pp. 153–154)

It's not just the number of businesses that has changed; it is also business's ability to compete. People used to view size as the determining factor in competitiveness, so that the larger the company, the larger its competitive advantage. In this environment, with the help of technology, a small, entrepreneurial business can potentially compete with a corporate giant.

Technology Is the Facilitator of Change

The impact of technology in the business world is perhaps most visible in e-mail and the Internet, but it goes far beyond those factors. Technology is the facilitator for products and services only science fiction writers envisioned in years past. It allows us to work across distances, and has created a new breed of worker—the free agent. It also catalyzes the rate of change in this environment.

The technology of the Internet is now an integral part of the business environment. Revenues from business-to-business sales over the Internet are in excess of $280 billion, and in spite of the recent shutdown of so many dot-coms, the Internet is not going to disappear as a business tool.

Employees Have More Choices

Today, employees have choices they never had before: They can choose to invest their time, energy, and talent in an enterprise; they can choose just to show up, to invest their time, but not to invest their knowledge; they can choose to take their knowledge to another organization. They can also choose from a wider variety of career paths.

As an article in *Management Review* so aptly observed: "Knowledge workers literally own the means of production. . . . Such employees are highly mobile because they change the balance of equity ownership—both in the company through stock options and in their own intellectual capital." (Weathersby, 1999, p. 7)

In the old economy, physical assets were king. Land, buildings, and machinery were how companies kept score. But in today's economy, intangibles like intellectual property, data, brand image, and know-how are the most valuable assets. With the move from physical assets to intangibles, the balance of power is shifting from the owners of land, buildings, and machinery (companies) to the owners of the intellect (employees). In the days of Scientific Management, employees were viewed as factors of production, like wooden pegs that could be easily moved from hole to hole, so one employee could be substituted for another. Companies did not worry about employee retention, except for a few employees who were designated as rising stars. But when a company is hiring minds, not just hands, they have to compete for unique, specialized talent. Hiring and retention become more critical.

Employees have more choices in their careers because the variety of job categories has increased tenfold. In the old, industrial economy, the number of official job categories (and career choices) was limited to about 80. Today, there are more than 800. In addition, employees have more choices about their employers: More companies mean more places to work and employees can choose based on the factors that are most important to them—size, culture, location, and so on.

Last, but certainly not least, employees can choose work that is enjoyable and meaningful. In the old days, people didn't expect to enjoy their work. Work was simply what had to be done to earn a paycheck. But today, employees expect work to be meaningful, and will change jobs or companies if those expectations are not met.

THE BRAIN-BASED BUSINESS WORLD

What do all of these changes mean? In my opinion, they point to one obvious conclusion. We're working in a brain-based business world.

Why do I say brain-based instead of knowledge-based? Because I believe that knowledge is too limited and too static. In this environment, it's not just what you know, but what you can create, implement, and communicate.

A brain-based business world means that for organizations and for individuals, thinking is no longer optional; it is essential. Because in this world, thinking is the new working capital.

It used to be that capital was narrowly defined, with the definition including tangible things like land, buildings, machinery, or money. In fact, the *American Heritage Dictionary* defines capital as "Wealth in the form of money or property, owned, used, or accumulated in business by an individual, partnership, or corporation." (Morris, 1985, p. 236) Today, we've come to recognize different types of capital—intellectual capital, human capital, innovation capital, and customer capital—all of which are connected to thinking.

So, thinking as working capital can be defined as wealth in the form of ideas, implementation skills, and working relationships invested or leveraged by an individual or organization.

Why is thinking the new working capital? Because knowledge work productivity—the primary work of this new brain-based world—requires the ability to generate ideas, which means people need to be able to think creatively, and to think differently. It requires the ability to implement ideas effectively, which means people need to make smart choices and be able to get things done. It also requires communicating well and creating good working relationships. All of these require effective thinking.

THE IMPLICATIONS OF A BRAIN-BASED BUSINESS WORLD FOR INDIVIDUALS

What does a brain-based business world mean to you and me as individuals in business? It means that to succeed in this new world, we need to *learn* to think more effectively, which includes learning how to change our thinking, how to generate ideas, how to get things done, and how to work with other people.

The good news is that if you invest in learning to think more effectively, you will not only increase your value to an employer, you will also make your working life easier, more fun, and less stressful. You will stop wasting time because you don't know how to jumpstart your brain. You will lower your stress and anxiety because you won't be a hostage to procrastination. You will enjoy being more creative and innovative. And you will reap the benefits of knowing how to build better working relationships.

Thinking puts the power in *your* hands instead of your employer's. It also gives you more clout in the job market. A business survey taken in the United Kingdom by PricewaterhouseCoopers in 1999 showed that organizations are now looking for creativity, communication skills, and adaptability in their employees.

There is no denying that technology has changed a lot of things in the business world. Although it is an incredible facilitator, it is no substitute for human thinking. Technology may improve the speed and ease of communication, but it cannot improve on fuzzy expression, poor content, or weak ideas. It can connect people electronically, but it cannot replace a person's ability to build a relationship.

Learning to change our thinking, generate ideas, get things done, and work with other people aren't skills that we were taught in school. They aren't skills that most people believed they needed to learn—until one day, the world changed. However, thinking skills are the new tools of the trade in this brain-based business world.

MANAGING ORGANIZATIONS IN A BRAIN-BASED BUSINESS WORLD

In a brain-based business world, organizations must be managed very differently than in the old, industrial economy. The assumptions on which policies, processes, and structure are based must change. The way in which organizations view employees, and the way that people are managed, must change. John Byrne, in his *Business Week* article on "The 21st Century Corporation," nailed it when he said: "To survive and thrive in this century, managers will need to hardwire a new set of rules and guideposts into their brains." (Byrne, 2000, p. 32)

First and foremost, organizations must become accustomed to investing in thinking, just as they are already accustomed to investing in land, buildings, and equipment. To compete, grow, and prosper in this brain-based world will require organizations to make investments in teaching employees how to think differently, how to generate ideas, how to get things done, and how to work effectively with other people. It will also require that organizations invest in encouraging employees to use those skills.

But there are three major perceptual barriers to investing in thinking skills. One barrier is that, for many organizations, thinking skills are categorized as "fluff" and therefore, unimportant. The second barrier is that organizations are reluctant to invest in something that can easily walk out the door (in the head of an employee). The third barrier is that just teaching the skills is not enough. Organizations also have to create a working environment that encourages employees to invest their thinking talent in the organization.

Investing in these fluff skills is not easy for many organizations to justify. Part of it is that these skills were not important in the old economy. And part of it may be that since thinking, communicating, and working with people are natural human processes that people do anyway—like breathing—organizations are unable to grasp the critical need to teach people how to do them better.

The scary part of investing in thinking skills is that, unlike physical assets, thinking resides in the brains of the employees. Because of that, employees can decide when and where to invest their thinking talent. Therefore, organizations need to see employees as investors, in the same way that stockholders are investors. And that means a whole different viewpoint about managing employees.

It also means that the working environment and culture of an organization are more important than ever before. Following the principles of Taylor-influenced management, which were developed for managing modular, repetitive tasks, squashes thinking instead of encouraging it. Attracting and retaining the best thinking talent and encouraging that thinking talent to invest in the organization takes more than just financial rewards. Organizations need to create an environment and culture that draws people in and makes them want to stay. These same organizations need to provide challenging opportunities that will engage the brains and hearts of thinking talent. Organizations that attract and retain the best thinking talent are what I call ThinkAble organizations—those that nurture and benefit from thinking.

Some of the characteristics of ThinkAble organizations are that they:

▌ Treat and reward employees as investors.

▌ Make it safe to learn and risk mistakes.

▌ Encourage alternate points of view.

▌ Share information.

▌ Encourage emotions.

▌ Use dialogue.

▌ Encourage informal networking.

▌ Discourage fear-based management.

▌ Value more than just numbers and financials.

▌ Dismantle hierarchy.

Unfortunately, most of these characteristics are in direct conflict with the ideas learned and practiced during the reign of Taylor-influenced management, and it is difficult for organizations to change long-held ideas, especially when the uncertainties of the new business world mean that there is no concrete proof that they must change.

2

THE ORIGINAL SEARCH ENGINE BRAIN

Remember that class you had in college—Principles of Brain Operation 101? The one where you learned about how people think, and how you can think more effectively? What, you don't remember that class?

That's probably because most people never had that class, or even one like it. Every student got a grounding in the principles of biology, physics, and math, as well as the events and lessons of history. You may have learned a bit about Freud, Pavlov, or Jung, but few people (unless you were a psychology major) learned much in school about the dynamics of human thinking. In fact, most people know more about how their computers operate than about how their brains operate.

In a brain-based business world, it is critical that people learn how to operate their brains effectively. In this chapter, you'll be introduced to my working metaphor for the brain, and learn about how your brain functions psychologically and physiologically. Understanding the Original Search Engine brain, and the concepts of psychology and physiology presented here provide a foundation for understanding the Brain Operating Principles and why they work as they do.

Every person has the potential to develop new ways of thinking and to break through thinking blocks. It is true that until recently scientists believed that once the brain completed its development during childhood, it stopped changing and growing. This belief led to the idea that learning was not important once a person finished school, the cautionary warnings about killing off brain cells, and the opinion that the ability to think degenerated with age. In fact, only in the past few years have scientists demonstrated that adults can generate new brain cells.

In this new environment, individuals and organizations need to change their old beliefs about learning, about aging, about thinking, and about change itself. It's time to debunk the myths that people cannot change, that people cannot learn to think better, and that people past the age of 65 cannot think and learn, because the reality of this new, brain-based environment is that no one can afford to squander brainpower.

WHY A SEARCH ENGINE?

There are a number of different metaphors that have been used to describe the brain. The most popular is the brain as computer. Scientists say that the metaphor of the brain as computer is not wholly accurate, because the brain is much more complex than even the most sophisticated computer. However, the reason that people make the comparison is that the brain shares some methods of information processing with computers.

I have my own working metaphor for the brain. Because of the ways people process information, instead of thinking of the brain as a computer, I think of it more as a search engine.

Almost everyone these days is familiar with Internet search engines, the tools that allow you to enter in a word, phrase, or question to find information or answers to your query. Your brain is the original search engine. Give it instructions, or ask it a question, and you send it on a quest for information. The big difference between an Internet search engine and your Original Search Engine (OSE) brain is that an Internet search engine has a designated boundary. Once it has found a certain numbers of answers to your inquiry, it stops searching and presents the information, organized according to some hierarchy. Your OSE brain, however, will continue the search until you instruct it differently. The OSE brain is also better than an Internet search engine at recognizing patterns and generalizing. A search through the contents of your brain will return much better information than one performed by an Internet search engine.

You have experienced this search capability if you have tried to remember the name of a person, and then hours or days later, the name popped onto your mental screen. You may have consciously forgotten that you were looking for the name, but your brain did not. It continued the search, while you went about your business.

I developed this metaphor of the OSE brain through a combination of observation, experience, and a fortuitous stumble across an explanation of auto-associative memory. Essentially, auto-associative memory means that when you ask for a piece of the concept you are searching for, your brain supplies you with the full concept. You provide a clue, and you get back the whole.

For this process to work, the brain has to be able to recognize pieces, or characteristics, of a concept, and not just the concept itself as a whole. In *How the Mind Works*, Steven Pinker explains piece recognition by showing how networks of neurons represent concepts. He says, ". . . both computers and brains represent concepts as *patterns* of activity over *sets* of units." Pinker illustrates by using the example of the category "vegetable." He points out that we think about a vegetable as a group of characteristics, and that each of those characteristics, or properties, can be stored as a separate bit, but also can be connected to the whole of the category. He says, "One bit might represent greenness, another leafiness, another crunchiness, and so on. Each of these vegetable-property units could be connected with a small weight to the vegetable unit itself. . . . Conceptually speaking, the more vegetable properties something has, the better example it is of a vegetable." (Pinker, 1999, pp. 101, 102)

Connecting the bits of information, or properties, is where auto-associative memories come in. Given one bit of information, the neural network automatically locates associated bits of information. An auto-associative network also has the ability to automatically complete a pattern based on part of the pattern. As Pinker says, ". . . the connections are redundant enough that even if only a *part* of the pattern for an item is presented to the auto-associator, say, greenness and crunchiness alone, the rest of the pattern, leafiness, gets completed automatically." (Pinker, 1999, p. 104) In addition to connecting the bits of associated information in patterns, the auto-associative network can generalize by making an inference that if two concepts are similar in some ways, they are probably similar in other ways.

Some brain scientists believe auto-associative memories are a key part of how people process information. Auto-associative memories don't tell the whole story, but they do explain a big part of it in a way that fits with what brain scientists know about how neural networks function.

Categories, which Pinker referred to, are also an important part of the thinking experience and how OSE brains function. Brains think in categories by stereotyping, by linking cause and effect, by associating, and by creating patterns. Antonio and Hanna Damasio, both professors of neurology, say that the brain ". . . categorizes the information so that related events and concepts—shapes, colors, trajectories in space and time, and pertinent body movements and reactions—can be reactivated together." (Damasio and Damasio, 1992, p. 91) This concept of categorization and reactivation explains why you can recognize people when they are in the context in which you know them—like the office—but you do not recognize them in an unfamiliar environment—like a restaurant. It also explains why you can remember a thought by retracing your steps, because the thought and the context are linked in your brain.

PSYCHOLOGY—THE SOFTWARE

To operate your brain effectively, it is helpful to understand some theories of psychology, the so-called software of the brain. There are several psychological theories and concepts that are useful in understanding how your brain works and that provide a basis for the Brain Operating Principles in *Brain Power*. These concepts include:

- *Selective attention:* the process of choosing what stimuli to pay attention to.
- *Schemas:* the framework people use to categorize what they know.
- *Cognitive consistency:* the desire to be (or appear to be) consistent.
- *Cognitive dissonance:* the discomfort produced when a person holds two conflicting beliefs.

Selective Attention

People are exposed to a flood of data every moment through their senses: color, shape, size, and movement from the eyes; volume, pitch, tone, and resonance from the ears; smells from the nose; taste from the mouth; and feelings of touch from the skin. If people had to pay attention to all of this data, their systems would overload and break down.

Instead, people filter information, deciding what to pay attention to and what to ignore. Selective attention is the process people use to decide what to pay attention to and what to block out. Information or stimuli are filtered on the basis of their meaning and relevance, and this filtering is a very individual process, because each person has his or her own unique filters.

Because of selective attention, everyone creates their own individual reality, based on how each person filters incoming stimuli. This is the reason that a group of people can experience the same event but remember and describe the event differently. Each person in the group chooses a different set of data to pay attention to, and therefore creates a uniquely different event.

Schemas

One of the ways your brain determines what to attend to and what to ignore is by using schemas, a concept that British psychologist Frederick Bartlett brought into the world of psychology in 1932. Schemas are organized patterns of knowledge about the world. Think of a schema like an old-fashioned pegboard—if the pegboard is your schema for *job*, for example, you would hang your rules and experiences about *job* on the pegs of the board. The pegboard (schema) provides a place for your brain to connect all of the rules and categories that turn experience into meaning. Schemas allow people to function without having all of the data all of the time. Imagine how complicated life would be if someone had to explain all of the rules and concepts that are attached to the idea of *job* every time they brought up the subject. Instead, once you have built your schema for *job*, you automatically associate it with concepts like working for a paycheck, having a boss, performing specific tasks, and so on. It is important to recognize that schemas generally operate unconsciously, so most of the time we are not aware of our schemas, even when they are functioning.

Schemas also guide attention. In *Vital Lies, Simple Truths*, Daniel Goleman explains the relationship between schemas and attention: "Schemas and attention interact in an intricate dance. Active attention arouses relevant schemas; schemas in turn guide the focus of attention. The vast repertoire of schemas lie dormant in memory, quiescent until activated by attention. Once active, they determine what aspects of the situation attention will track. . . .

Schemas not only determine what we will notice: they also determine what we do *not* notice [his emphasis]." (Goleman, 1986, pp. 79–80) In other words, what you pay attention to and what you filter out are the result of your own personalized schemas.

Cognitive Consistency and Dissonance

Another psychological concept that underlies the Brain Operating Principles in this book is cognitive consistency. Cognitive consistency is the desire to be (and appear to others) consistent in words and behavior. Some social psychologists believe that the need for consistency is a central motivator for human behavior.

The significance of cognitive consistency is in how it affects people's thoughts and behavior, particularly their decisions. In his book, *Influence*, Robert Cialdini warns that "The drive to be (and look) consistent constitutes a highly potent weapon of social influence, often causing us to act in ways that are clearly contrary to our own best interests." He adds, "If I can get you to make a commitment (that is, to take a stand, to go on record), I will have set the stage for your automatic and ill-considered consistency with that earlier commitment. Once a stand is taken, there is a natural tendency to behave in ways that are stubbornly consistent with that stand. (Cialdini, 1993, pp. 59, 67) In other words, because of cognitive consistency, people will agree to requests or statements they would not otherwise agree to, or behave in a way they otherwise wouldn't—just so that they can be (or appear to be) consistent.

One of the reasons that people desire to be consistent is because of what is called cognitive dissonance, which is created when people are not consistent. Leon Festinger introduced the theory of cognitive dissonance in the 1950s, and it became one of the most influential theories in social psychology. The theory states that whenever a person holds two ideas, beliefs, attitudes, or opinions that are in conflict (or a thought and a behavior that are in conflict) the person will experience the discomfort of dissonance, and will be motivated to change one of the conflicting thoughts or actions to reduce the dissonance. Elliot Aronson modified Festinger's theory of cognitive dissonance in the late 1960s, suggesting that "dissonance is most powerful in situations in which the self-concept is threatened." (Aronson, 1998, p. 211)

The discomfort of dissonance motivates people to find a way to reduce it. There are several strategies people use to reduce dissonance:

▌ Change one or more of the dissonant ideas, beliefs, attitudes, opinions, or behaviors.

▌ Reduce the importance of one of the dissonant elements.

▌ Seek out information to confirm one side of the dissonance.

▌ Distort or misinterpret the information involved.

Therefore, in the drive to reduce dissonance, people may rationalize behavior, distort information, or even screen out dissonant messages, which accounts for behavior that may seem inexplicable or erratic to others.

The theories of cognitive consistency and dissonance apply in many areas, such as information processing, persuasion, selling, and motivation; however, they are especially influential in decision making. For example, following a significant decision, people will almost always experience dissonance. This is because when someone makes a choice, the benefits of the choice made rarely outweigh the other possibilities so strongly that the decision is not made without some equivocation. To deal with the dissonance following a significant decision, Aronson says, "people tend to focus on the positive aspects of their choices and to downplay the attractive qualities of the unchosen alternatives." Aronson also notes, " . . . when a decision is irrevocable, more dissonance is aroused; to reduce this dissonance, people become more certain they are right *after* there is nothing they can do about it." (Aronson, 1998, pp. 195, 199)

THE PHYSIOLOGY OF THINKING AND LEARNING

If you are not a big fan of science, you might be tempted to skip this section. I urge you not to give in to temptation. My goal here is to provide a basic understanding of the physiology of thinking. Why is it important for you to understand the basic physiology of the brain? Because understanding the physiology is part of understanding how to operate your brain so that you can think and learn more effectively.

It is also important because in this rapidly changing business environment, learning to change your thinking is critical for success. And changing your thinking is easier once you learn the processes involved.

Thinking Connections

It is an interesting parallel that the key to success in this chaotic business world is itself chaotic. Scientists used to think that the brain was a logical, linear, neatly organized system. Now, with the knowledge gained through new technology, scientists view the brain as a complex, chaotic network. The connections between neurons in this network are the key to thinking. To understand the importance of connections, it is useful to understand a little about how neurons work. In *A User's Guide to the Brain*, Dr. John Ratey explains that the brain is an:

> . . . *overgrown jungle of 100 billion nerve cells, or neurons, which begin as round cell bodies that grow processes called axons and dendrites. Each nerve cell has one axon and as many as 100,000 dendrites. Dendrites are the main way by which neurons get information (learn); and axons are the main way by which neurons pass on information to (teach) other neurons. The neuron and its thousands of neighbors send out roots and branches—the axons and dendrites— in all directions, which intertwine to form an interconnected tangle with 100 trillion constantly changing connections. There are more possible ways to connect the brain's neurons than there are atoms in the universe. [Ratey, 2001, pp. 19–20]*

As Ratey suggests in this passage, you can think of the axon as a root and dendrites as branches. The branchlike dendrites stretch toward, but don't actually touch, the axons of one or more neurons. The microscopic gap between an axon and dendrites is called the synapse (or, technically, the synaptic cleft). Connections happen when neurotransmitters, a group of chemicals, carry messages back and forth across synapses. The strength or weakness of the connection is what scientists refer to as synaptic strength.

Thinking, sensing, movement, and so on happen because of those connections among neurons. Groups of neurons on the surface of the cerebral cortex process information from sense organs and nerves, and the neurons communicate messages, chemically and electrically, to other areas of the brain (as well as to the muscles and organs of the body).

Thinking is not just a process of connecting one single neuron to another. Neurons connect in patterns across the brain. Neurology professors Antonio and Hanna Damasio refute the traditional concept of thinking in pictures, and explain how these patterns of connections represent an idea: "We believe there are no permanently held 'pictorial' representations of objects or persons as was traditionally thought. Instead, the brain holds, in effect, a record of the neural activity that takes place in the sensory and motor cortices during interaction with a given object. The records are patterns of synaptic connections that can recreate the separate sets of activities that define an object or event; each record can stimulate related ones." (Damasio and Damasio, 1992, p. 91) The synaptic connections to which the Damasios refer are scattered across many different parts of the cerebral cortex. So what you sense or think isn't stored in just one location in the brain.

A pattern of synaptic connections represents your experience with something, whether it is an object, a person, an emotion, a thought, or a movement. When these patterns are repeated, they are strengthened, enabling you to learn and remember. The technical name for this process is long-term potentiation (LTP). Ratey explains the physiology of LTP: "As neurons in the chain strengthen their bonds with one another, they then begin to recruit neighboring neurons to join the effort. Each time the activity is repeated, the bonds become a little stronger, and more neurons become involved, so that eventually an entire network develops that remembers the skill, the word, the episode, or the color. At this stage, the subject becomes encoded as memory." (Ratey, 2001, pp. 190–191) Long-term potentiation is why, as a child, you were told that practice makes perfect. As you repeated a new behavior or idea, you brain was building the connections it needed. It is also why both change and learning require practice and perseverance.

Your Uniquely Wired Brain

The physiological and psychological processes of thinking are something we all have in common. No matter what your education, your professional experience, or your job, the processes work the same—as do the Brain Operating Principles in *Brain Power*, which are based on those processes.

Although the processes and principles may be the same for all of us, the outcomes are different. The events of your life create the connections in your brain, so your patterns of synaptic connections are different from anyone else's. Since no one has exactly the same experiences of the world as another, each person has a uniquely wired brain. For example, the pattern that the word *business* activates in your brain is different from the one it activates in someone else's. And the same goes for other words: boss, employee, leadership, commitment, work, job, productivity, and so on.

The processes and principles help us to see the similarities in how people think and to understand some of the differences. They also help us learn to appreciate the differences, which is important because it is the differences that define our individuality.

3

BRAIN OPERATING PRINCIPLE 1: Bermuda Triangles of Information

Given a black hole of information, people will fill the hole with negative conclusions

Nature has some peculiar ways of trying to protect us. One is to push our nervous systems and OSE brains toward the negative when we are confronted with uncertainty. As evolutionary psychologists would say, it is a holdover from the days when fight or flight was the critical instinct for survival. Today, the fight or flight instinct still weighs in when we are reacting to uncertainty or to a stressful situation. It influences our brains toward the negative.

This negativity bias is the basis for the principle of Bermuda Triangles of Information: Given a black hole (or lack) of information or communication, people will fill the hole with negative conclusions. In fact, the conclusions are often much more negative than reality.

The name of the principle is borrowed from the geographic region off the southeastern Atlantic coast of the United States, called the Bermuda or Devil's Triangle, which is legendary as a black hole, where strange and terrible things happen to people in boats and planes. Stories are told about the sudden loss of radio contact, compasses that spin for no reason, and the planes, small boats, and ships that have disappeared in the area. Because of the lack of information or explanation about these unusual occurrences, the geographic Bermuda Triangle has become a magnet for stories about the supernatural, the mysterious, and the threatening. Thus, I have formed the psychological link between the rumors and legends of this seamark and its namesake, the Brain Operating Principle that compels people to fill in black holes with negative conclusions.

Every mother has experienced this principle. When a child is late coming home, what do mothers think first? The young one was having too much fun and lost track of time? No. With the black hole of a missing child and no phone call, the mother assumes the worst: There was an accident, and her child is clinging to life by a thread, identified only as a John or Jane Doe, in a hospital emergency room.

EVERYDAY TRIANGLES

You do not need to look very far to find the potential for black holes in your everyday working life. They show up whenever there is uncertainty or a lack of communication. Perhaps you've found yourself in this situation at work: One of your colleagues is exhibiting signs of frustration, irritation, or anger. Maybe she slams some papers down on the desk or you ask her a question and receive a curt response. You think, "Uh-oh, what did I do or say?" instead of thinking, "She's having a bad day." You fill the black hole with the assumption that her anger is directed at you, even if you can think of nothing specific you did to provoke it.

For instance, two of my clients, Mark and Joan, are business partners. During a recent stressful period at work, Joan began to show signs of irritation and anger. Mark started walking around on eggshells, assuming that he had said or done something to upset her. When the three of us sat down to examine the business situation, Mark was surprised and relieved to learn that Joan's bad mood was a result of stress from the business and wasn't intentionally directed at him.

ANXIETY TRIANGLES

Bermuda Triangles can create anxiety when there is an unknown. When the outcome of a situation is in doubt, we tend to anticipate the negative and, therefore, create anxiety about what will happen. Rarely do we have a positive expectation when an outcome is in question.

The arrival of a new boss is a classic example of an unknown quantity creating a black hole and the resulting anxiety. One employee, observing the impact of a new boss in her company, described how the anxiety was causing people to perform the equivalent of circus tricks:

Thirteen Situations That Create Bermuda Triangles

1. Layoffs.
2. Restructuring.
3. New initiatives.
4. New people (especially new management).
5. Gain or loss of a client/customer.
6. Annual review time.
7. Closed doors.
8. Cost-cutting.
9. Telecommuting/distance work/branch offices.
10. Unexpected meetings.
11. New products.
12. Process reengineering.
13. Geographic/location moves.

jugglers (juggling too many projects), clowns (using humor to relieve the tension), acrobats (taking public risks), and lion tamers (taking on the impossible problems). In addition to the circus tricks, think of the rumors that fly when a new boss arrives on the scene. How often do the rumors take a positive spin, such as the potential for promotion, exciting new projects, or improved atmosphere? Not very often, right? Usually the rumors are related to the fears that surface about the possible changes that will be imposed by the new person—job changes, loss of status, or even unemployment.

Sales professionals are prone to anxiety triangles when an inevitable slow period arrives, particularly after a busy time. They might fear that the slowdown is the beginning of a downward slide to no business, instead of just a temporary event. Most businesses have natural cycles of busy and not-so-busy periods of time, but sometimes it is hard to remember that it is part of the cycle when a slow period arrives.

A slow period can become a big, black hole with negative

assumptions for small business owners who don't have cash re-
serves. For an individual who relies on month-to-month cash flow
to stay afloat, a slow month feels longer and more sinister than it is.
Since no one can predict when the slow period will end, the tendency is to assume it is a trend and not just a temporary occurrence.

Bermuda Triangles of the unknown also occur when we feel
overwhelmed by an undefined amount of work that is due by a specific deadline. When the extent of the work is not well defined, the
tendency toward negativity makes a project seem bigger than it is.
When I find myself overwhelmed by work, my strategy is to force myself to sit down and close the hole by laying out the work and making
a list of the tasks to be accomplished. Once I do this, the anxiety disappears. It is tempting to resist making the list because it takes time I
don't think I have, but ever since I recognized this situation as a
Bermuda Triangle, I know I will function more effectively when I fill
in the black hole.

Once this version of a Bermuda Triangle became evident to me, I
began to see it among some of the clients I coach. One client was
amazed by the difference this simple strategy made in reducing her
feeling of being out of control. Janet spent the first part of our coaching
session talking about all of the things she should have been doing, but
did not have time to do. She then spent the second part of the session
talking about how stressed she was. It soon became clear that a
Bermuda Triangle of the unknown was operating. We scheduled an
emergency session and I worked with her to draw out all of the tasks
and projects she had on her mind. We used 3M's Post-it Notes to prioritize the work by laying it out on the wall. Once the projects were laid
out in black and white (or black and yellow in this case), the black
hole was closed and Janet's anxiety diminished as she regained a sense
of control over her workload.

VIRTUAL TRIANGLES

Bermuda Triangles often affect people who work together across
distances. Telecommuters and branch office workers are particularly
at risk. Black holes can affect the perception of their performance,
their working relationships, and their job satisfaction. When people
are absent physically from one another, it is easy for negative trian-

gles to develop on either side. In this case, out of sight equals out of favor.

Managers who are responsible for workers who telecommute or work in separate offices are prone to negative assumptions about productivity, responsibility, and commitment. First, managers cannot help but wonder if a distance worker is working as hard as those in the office. "What are they doing when I'm not watching them?" is a common concern. Second, managers tend to be more nervous about whether a distance worker will meet deadlines. Since a manager cannot see a distance worker actually at work on a project, it's difficult to trust that a project is on schedule. Third, managers are quicker to question the commitment of an employee who is not physically present. The manager doesn't see the constant choices made by a distance worker to put the job first, unlike employees who are seen face to face. When a distance worker calls in sick, needs to reschedule an on-site meeting, or asks to push back a due date, managers might assume the employee's commitment to the job is wavering.

Black holes also affect the perceptions of distance workers about their managers and their organizations. For people who are absent from the daily hubbub of an organization, the business environment can seem pretty quiet. They miss chance meetings, hallway conversations, and spontaneous brainstorms. When they are not getting regular news about the office activities, workers might assume that something negative is happening. Because distance workers are disconnected from the everyday operations and conversations, it is also more difficult for them to gauge how they are performing in relation to the business, or if they are meeting managers' expectations.

People who work in branch offices share similar concerns. Branch offices often have a second-class-citizen feeling. People in these offices can miss out on opportunities, feel cut off from resources, and feel less important to the business than those who work at a headquarters office. Even though these factors may not be true, the perception can be a powerful force in the attitude and job satisfaction of branch workers.

Individuals who telecommute or work in separate offices from their bosses can prevent Bermuda Triangles by setting up a system to keep their bosses informed and involved in their projects. If you are

physically separated from your boss, plan to update your boss regularly with a short report that lists what projects you are working on,
what you have accomplished, and where you might need her help. It's
important to regularly reassure your boss that you are on track to meet
your deadlines. It's also important to make sure your boss is aware of
your contributions: when you work overtime, when you help out a
colleague, when you go above and beyond in your job. Because those
contributions are more likely to be invisible than the contributions of
your counterparts who are physically in the office, it is critical that you
toot your own horn. The perception that keeping people informed is
the same as bragging is part of what keeps distance workers from filling those black holes. People who were taught not to brag are uncomfortable with communicating when it seems like boasting. Instead,
they hope that someone else will just notice their accomplishments so
they do not have to be the ones to bring the work to the attention of
others. Another reason people don't typically follow through on con-
tinuous communication is that it takes extra time that no one has to
spare. So, getting work done becomes the priority in the time available;
selling themselves is not.

Branch managers who supervise people that are disconnected
from the headquarters office can prevent Bermuda Triangles through
communication, too. Branch managers should have someone in the
headquarters office who keeps them informed about what's happening, so information can be passed on to the people in the branch office. An important ingredient to prevent the feeling of being a
second-class-citizen is to build a sense of community in the branch.
Branch managers can also prevent this second-class feeling by en-
suring their employees are informed of job openings, that their work
is recognized by bosses in the headquarters office, and by putting re-
source constraints in the context of similar constraints experienced
by the headquarters' staff.

Bosses in these situations must be aware of the potential for black
holes and close them before they develop. One administrative support
person can be assigned to send copies of interoffice memos to distance
workers and branch managers. That same person can be designated as
the liaison with distance workers, assuring regular contact. The boss
may not have time to call routinely, but if someone from his office
does, employees will feel that headquarters cares about them, thereby
closing potential black holes.

COMMUNICATE TO PREVENT BLACK HOLES

The principle of Bermuda Triangles of Information illustrates how important it is for leaders and managers to communicate regularly. In the absence of regular communication, rumors, misinformation, and negative assumptions develop in employees' minds. The more fear and uncertainty in an environment, the more negative the rumors and gossip will be.

Most leaders are operating under the illusion that they communicate more often than they actually do. They also labor under the illusion that if they have said something once, they do not need to say it again. Communicating regularly, whether it is company-wide or person to person, is one of the most overlooked methods of building trust, developing relationships, encouraging loyalty, creating a sense of involvement, and, by the way, of preventing Bermuda Triangles and their effects.

Pick up any business magazine, and you will see employee retention cited as one of the top concerns of business leaders. *Fortune* magazine interviewed three of the nation's top executive recruiters, asking them to describe the competition for talent from the recruiters' perspective. When asked what advice they would give companies to retain the best executives, the three recruiters recommended communication, appreciation, and rewards.

The importance of communication and feedback are underestimated by organizations. In fact, a 1999 survey by *The Wall Street Journal* showed that poor communication, unclear expectations, and a lack of feedback on performance were three of the top reasons that people leave their jobs.

It is a rare manager who communicates frequently and comprehensively enough that employees don't form black holes about their performance, the value of their contribution, or their future prospects in the company. Even star performers can be uncertain about their status and start looking for opportunities where their hard work and ideas will be better appreciated. The uncertainty makes a new job look very appealing, especially when the recruiter expresses admiration for the candidate's achievements and skills and emphasizes the new company's strengths and opportunities.

Here is a good rule of thumb for preventing Bermuda Triangles. One of the keys to sustaining an effective relationship is to have a

5:1 ratio of positive to negative feedback. That means five positive or appreciative comments to each negative one. The 5:1 ratio prevents Bermuda Triangles by increasing both the amount and quality of feedback.

MAKING UNFAMILIAR RISKS FAMILIAR

Bermuda Triangles can develop when we're worried about an unfamiliar and risky situation that will take place in the future, such as a meeting, presentation, interview, or performance. The unknown aspects of the situation, together with apprehension about the risks of the event,

---

ACTION TOOL: The 5:1 Feedback Ratio

Experiment with the 5:1 ratio of positive to negative feedback. Try it with the person who frustrates you the most. If you are brave, tackle the five-a-day approach—that's five appreciative comments per day. If five-a-day sounds like a lot, a less intimidating approach is to work your way up to five each day by starting with five each week. Most people don't need to plan for the negative feedback; it comes as a natural part of the working process.

Here are a few appreciative phrases and ideas to get you started:

I "You did a great job on . . . project."
I "I appreciate the way you. . ."
I "Thank you for the job you did yesterday."
I "I appreciate your upbeat attitude."
I "I appreciate the way you. . ."
I "I do not tell you enough what a great job you do."
I Write a short note and mail it or put it on someone's desk.
I Bring a small plant as a thank-you.
I Put a candy bar, a movie theatre ticket, or bubble gum on the person's desk.

combine to push our brains to imagine negative outcomes. In the case of one of my clients, the prospect of giving a formal speech to a committee at work was causing considerable anxiety. The client, Natalie, was accustomed to giving informal presentations during weekly meetings with her immediate colleagues. Trying to prepare for the new, unfamiliar risk, Natalie's mind developed a Bermuda Triangle. Her runaway brain imagined failure: rejection of her ideas by the audience and ridicule. A week before the speech, Natalie was tense and almost hyperventilating as she shared her fears with me.

I recommended that Natalie start mentally rehearsing the presentation with a more positive outcome. The mind doesn't know the difference between something we visualize and something we physically experience, so the process of visualizing (mentally rehearsing) acquaints the brain with an unfamiliar situation and closes those black holes. Also, if you visualize it repeatedly, the actual experience isn't as strange, awkward, or intimidating as when you experience something for the first time.

The process of visualization I taught to Natalie and to many other business professionals is a system for success that athletes also use to improve their performance under pressure. You can use the technique to build your confidence and improve your performance on a sales call, job interview, or when you are scheduled to make an important presentation. Visualizing is easy; it's like daydreaming with a purpose.

To visualize a presentation, close your eyes and imagine your presentation as if you were watching a movie. See yourself walking into the room with confidence. Watch yourself as you deliver your presentation flawlessly. Note how your audience laughs and applauds at just the right moments. Then, imagine the appreciative reactions of your audience—their applause and admiring comments. Feel your pride and satisfaction at a job well done. Run through your performance like you are watching a movie, but make sure you feel the feelings as well as see the visuals. Once you see it in your mind, you can make it happen in the physical world.

Natalie reported that the visualization tool produced immediate results, significantly lowering her stress level about the performance. She was amazed at how similar her actual presentation was to the visualization she had practiced, and thrilled at the success of her presentation.

ORGANIZATIONAL BERMUDA TRIANGLES

Organizations run the risk of creating Bermuda Triangles with their customers when they neglect to communicate or to provide sufficient information during or after the sale. When a lack of information occurs, customers are compelled by their Original Search Engine brains to fill the black holes with negative conclusions. The negative conclusions can frustrate or anger your customers, or even worse, they can result in customers choosing to do business with another company in the future.

Let's say you are a supplier and one of your customers is waiting for a certain product to be available. How you handle this situation can affect the way your customer feels about your company and the prospect of repeat business—often more than the speed with which you fill the order.

In this situation, companies may wait until they have concrete news—a definitive delivery date or significant progress—to communicate with the customer. But that lack of information in between leaves a black hole that is easy for your customer to fill with a negative, such as, "There is a problem with the product"; "They lost my order"; or "They do not care about my business." A strategy of filling the hole with repeated information by reconfirming the projected delivery date, or a reassurance that everything is still on schedule, can make the difference between an angry, anxious customer and a pleased, satisfied one.

The effectiveness of this kind of communication strategy is not limited to situations where a customer is waiting for a product that is back-ordered. It also works in situations where a product has a long production timeline, when delivery is scheduled over a period of time, or when there is a long lag time between order and delivery.

Organizations also create black holes with customers when they don't explain the technical aspects of a transaction to customers. These include explaining the working process, as well as defining technical language and jargon. Unknowns about the technical aspects of a transaction create uncertainty for a customer, which also increases a customer's risk in doing business with the organization. Most organizations just assume that because the process or jargon is second nature to them, it is also obvious to their customers.

Whether it is a lack of information about the status of an order, a lack of information about working processes, or a lack of knowledge about the technical aspects of a business, each of these situations has something in common—an opportunity for black holes to develop and customers to fill them in with the negative.

SILENCE IS NOT GOLDEN

When it comes to managing what public relations practitioners call issues, there is one phrase that describes the best way to handle information that impacts the public: "Tell it all and tell it now." However, for companies facing a public issue, such as a product recall, contamination, or faulty work, the typical reaction is to defer releasing any information. Instead, internal investigations of the situation are undertaken, and many discussions and meetings take place to weigh the alternatives of discovery versus disclosure: the possibility of an outside person discovering the situation versus the unpleasant aftermath of disclosing the information.

Releasing the information promptly allows a company to control its release and how the issue is presented. Waiting to release information, hoping that the media won't discover the story, means that when the information does hit the news, the company appears more at fault, and the situation appears more sinister because it is presumed the company is hiding something. By holding back information, the company creates the opportunity for black holes and their negative effects. The public wonders: "What other, even more terrible things is this company not telling us?"

Intel fell victim to Bermuda Triangles in 1994, when customers discovered that Intel's Pentium chip could be mathematically inaccurate in large calculations. The incident, triggered by a math professor's discovery, was discussed in several postings at an Internet site before it was acknowledged by the company. The professor declared the mathematical capabilities of the chip flawed, based on the fact that he had detected a division error while studying complex math problems. Intel already knew about the problem in the chip, had studied it, and calculated that the average spreadsheet user would only run into the problem once every 27,000 years. Reassured that the flaw would not affect most users, Intel set about developing and testing ways to correct the defect. Intel failed, however, to inform consumers of the problem and communicate that it was working on a solution. The industry press picked up the story. Then the general consumer media, led by CNN, leaped to fill in the hole with negative coverage.

Intel originally offered to replace the problem chip for any user who regularly performed complex mathematical calculations. As a result of the media stories and the ensuing public outcry, Intel was eventually forced to replace the problem chip for every single customer who requested it. Because of the black holes of information, consumers assumed the problem was worse than it was, causing millions to request the replacement chip. Intel lost credibility in the marketplace and its prodigious 75 percent market share began to slip away. The company also took a $475 million write-off to replace parts and pull materials off the production line. If Intel had informed consumers of the problem up front, chances are that these costs could have been significantly lower, saving Intel millions.

To summarize, Intel handled the chip problem in perfect alignment with their technical/scientific culture. They identified a problem, mathematically assessed the probability of it occurring, and set about developing a solution. Unfortunately, like many other companies who find themselves in the public eye, Intel failed to inform consumers of the problem and their efforts to fix it, thereby causing a Bermuda Triangle of Information to develop. In this technological environment, where information can be shared across the world with a few keystrokes, companies cannot afford to ignore the potential for Bermuda Triangles.

GOOD STRATEGY . . . BAD EXECUTION

A good idea is valuable, but if it's not well executed, it can lose its value and even cause harm. When a good strategy goes bad in the execution, look for Bermuda Triangles—especially the triangles that form when companies fail to put themselves in the shoes of their customers.

All too often, companies implement programs based on an internal viewpoint of the world, failing to consider how their customers might perceive the program, or the different (sometimes radically different) world in which their customers live. For example, one day, while I was on a business trip, I received a voice-mail message: "This is so-and-so from your bank, could you please call me at your earliest convenience at this number?"

Because this message provided little information, my first thought was that there was a problem with my bank account. Concerned, I returned the call from the airport, only to have the person on the other end say, "I was just calling to thank you for being our customer."

The idea of making the call was a nice gesture. Unfortunately, because of the principle of Bermuda Triangles, the call had the opposite effect. By not telling me the nature of the call, I assumed the worst. Had the caller left me a voice-mail message, saying something like, "This is so-and-so from your bank and we'd like to thank you for being our customer. Please call us whenever we can be of assistance to you," the bank would have conveyed their positive message, and I would have received it in the same way.

To prevent black holes when you are communicating with your customers, ask yourself:

▌ What questions will customers have that are not answered in this communication?

▌ Is there anything that could be misunderstood?

▌ What can I do to make this information as clear and complete as possible?

One technique for testing your communication is to ask someone who is not familiar with the program to read the information and list the questions that come to mind. Then, ensure that those questions, however basic, are answered in the information.

TRIANGLES AND WAITS

During waiting periods, Bermuda Triangles can easily develop. Even if you are in an industry that traditionally has a specified waiting period, the new, frenetic business environment may have shifted customers' viewpoints without your noticing. Today, with FedEx, faxes, cell phones, e-mail, voice mail, and the Internet, people are accustomed to fast, if not instant response. So, our frame of reference for time periods has shortened considerably.

In the past, waiting two to three weeks for the production of a product was customary. Today, even two to three days without information can seem like a long time and can create Bermuda Triangles. Customers can fill these holes with negative perceptions like, "They've lost my order" or "There's something wrong and I will not make my deadline" or "Maybe this company does not know what it is doing."

As a frequent flyer, I've experienced firsthand how frustrating and avoidable Bermuda Triangles created by delays can be.

On a trip through the Baltimore-Washington International airport, the plane we were supposed to take to Orlando developed mechanical problems and a new plane was needed. This is not an unusual problem and is one people can accept and understand. However, the problem was not announced to the passengers in the boarding area until 20 minutes before take-off, after several people had asked about the status of the flight. The staff finally explained the problem over the P.A. system and posted a new departure time of one hour later.

Unfortunately, the plane we needed was stuck in Chicago because of storms. Again, not an unusual situation. However, the airline staff continued to stick to the new departure time of one hour, even though the plane had not yet left the ground in Chicago. Four hours later, we finally took off, but the constant lack of information caused passengers to fill the holes with negative possibilities, such as, "Will we have to spend the night here?" and "Will I miss my meeting tomorrow morning?" When we did take off, it was with a load of frustrated and angry passengers.

The conclusion: airlines could drastically improve customer satisfaction simply by anticipating black holes.

ACTION TOOL: Conduct an External Bermuda Triangles Scan

Use the questions and situations opposite to identify the Bermuda Triangles your company is creating with customers.

ACTION TOOL: Conduct an External
Bermuda Triangles Scan *(Continued)*

Questions to Help You Identify Bermuda Triangles:

1. What are your customer's contact points with your company?
2. Are any rumors circulating in your industry about your company or your products?
3. What information do your customers have and not have that they need to have?
4. Could your customers be receiving conflicting information? From where?
5. What due dates or milestones are involved?
6. When was the last time you communicated with your customers and what was it about?
7. At what point do you explain your company's working process to your customers? What parts of the process require a customer's input or participation?
8. Where do you use jargon or technical language in your verbal or written communication? Is it on your Web site? In your sales brochures? In the owner's manuals? A part of your technical support language?

Eleven Situations That Create Bermuda Triangles for Customers:

1. A complex project in progress.
2. A customer just signed a contract (buyer's remorse).
3. Changes in your management or client team.
4. A problem with your product/service.
5. A customer waiting for delivery.
6. A customer waiting for a report or call back.
7. Changes in delivery dates or milestones.
8. A customer just placed an order and has not received confirmation.
9. Changes in your company (talked about in the media or industry gossip).
10. New product introductions.
11. Mystery processes.

E-EXPECTATIONS

E-expectations are the expectations that we can also perform instantaneously since we can communicate instantaneously, because of technology and the Internet. E-expectations appear when we fail to allow a realistic amount of time for completion of a request.

The advent of electronic information at our fingertips has shortened the patience span of customers, particularly when dealing with service requests. Today, it seems to take very little to send a customer into a tirade, and dealing with an irate customer is never pleasant. You can soothe irritation or even prevent indignation by managing expectations:

I If customers call for service, explain the process and give them a timeline.

I If your customers need information and you cannot provide it immediately, give them a time estimate of when they can expect your response (and meet it).

I If you are part way through a project, don't wait for completion; give your client updates along the way.

I When you do give time frames, remember the old saying: "Underpromise and overdeliver."

A property management company had e-expectations causing major problems in their business. This company, which had been very successful for years, found that several new customer service managers were failing to respond to customer voice-mail messages until they could either perform the requested tasks or verify the information needed. The requests included things like non-emergency repairs to a property, information about the rental status of their property, or inquiring about the status of a check. The customers had e-expectations, so when they didn't get an immediate return call, creating a black hole, they called again and again, some growing repeatedly incensed and even verbally abusive when they did not get the response they expected. The company's call load tripled, which created an even higher stress level for the employees and the owners.

To close the black holes, the company began managing their customer's expectations by promising to respond to requests within 24 hours, they increased the use of e-mail and when they couldn't solve a problem right away, they started calling customers to tell them when they could expect the request to be completed or the information to be verified. The company is now running smoother than ever, the stress level is lower, productivity and profits are up, and everyone is happier.

CREATING UNCERTAINTY

One of the strategies some companies like to use with customers is to deliberately obscure their working processes. Advertising agencies and similar service providers are often particularly mysterious about the process of their work, and they heighten the mystery by using what they call *proprietary processes*.

Perhaps your company does not go to these lengths, but not explaining the work process to your customers can have the same effect as deliberately creating a mystery. Remember that just because the process is second nature to you doesn't mean that it is obvious to your customer. It may be the first time the customer has worked with a business like yours. The customer could be new to her job. Or, your company may work differently than another company in the same field.

Companies also create black holes of uncertainty by using jargon or technical language. People use jargon and technical language for several reasons: first, they believe the language marks them as experts; second, because they assume the customer knows what they are talking about; or third, because the jargon or technical language is second nature to them, it slides naturally into conversation.

Jargon and mystery processes both create uncertainty for customers. The less customers understand, the less sure they will be about working with you. When customers are unsure, their perception of the risk of doing business with your company increases. Customers can find ways around your mystery and jargon—by finding another company to provide the services or products needed. To avoid losing customers, develop flow charts or other printed explanations of your work processes and give customers timelines for feedback throughout the process.

It is easy to forget and use jargon in conversations outside of the business when you are accustomed to using the language in internal conversations. One way to raise awareness about jargon and technical language in conversation is to play buzzword bingo in internal meetings. Make a list of your common buzzwords and phrases. Then have people put a quarter in the pot when someone catches them using a buzzword bingo word.

TRIANGLE PREVENTION

Look around you and identify where you can prevent Bermuda Triangles from forming in your business. Search for opportunities to update your customers on status, on changes, or just to tell them the work is progressing. Explain the process of the work and avoid or define jargon and technical language.

Disney uses the Bermuda Triangles principle brilliantly with the lines at its theme parks. Approximate waiting times are clearly marked at junctures along the way, so you know if you can expect a 40-minute wait, a 20-minute wait, or just a five-minute wait. Of course, the line always moves faster than the sign promised. And rarely do you stand in line without something to look at or entertain you.

In addition, companies can prevent Bermuda Triangles by investing in technology that lets customers track the status of their orders online or by telephone. When customers have the opportunity to access information, they are less prone to the effects of black holes. Customer satisfaction increases, and employees spend less time answering queries about the status of an order.

The principle of Bermuda Triangles is especially important for Web-based business practices. Companies that are succeeding with Web-based transactions have built good business practices for communicating with their customers. The move from tangible transactions (in person or by phone) to electronic ones means that confirmation of an order is a critical step in limiting the potential for black holes, especially because technological glitches sometimes send electronic messages into oblivion.

Amazon.com has developed first-rate processes for preventing black holes in a business that is vulnerable to Bermuda Triangles. Amazon.com first sends an e-mail confirming the order and providing details for how to check on its status. Next, they send another e-mail to say the order was shipped and estimate when delivery can be expected.

They even keep customers updated with a we're-still-looking e-mail when an extended search for an out-of-print book is underway.

Not every business has the short time frame of an Amazon.com. What if your business is one that takes longer than a few days before an order can be fulfilled? Follow the example of a company called Modern Postcard. Customers of Modern Postcard can choose to receive daily e-mail updates, informing them of the current status of their postcard order, the expected time frame, and the next step in the process. One example of an e-mail update is captured below.

> *"Your order has been plated and is waiting to be printed. It is scheduled to print on Monday, January 22, 2001. Your order will most likely be shipped the next business day after printing. Please keep in mind that printing dates may be delayed due to mechanical failure, illness, or production problems. Your order is being shipped by DHL Express, which is an overnight service in most areas. You will be notified with an Estimated Arrival Date when the order is completed."*

Modern Postcard's process is only a few weeks, but this type of status reporting could easily be adapted for projects that take even longer. In every business, there is an opportunity to proactively inform customers about the process. Even businesses that traditionally don't talk much to their customers can benefit from thinking through their processes and identifying opportunities to explain the process to customers.

KEY POINTS

▎ Given a black hole (or lack) of information or communication, people will fill the hole with negative conclusions.

▎ The nervous system and OSE brain lean toward the negative.

▎ When the outcome of a situation is in doubt, Bermuda Triangles develop and create anxiety; fill the hole with specific information or visualization.

▎ Telecommuting and distance work can create black holes and negative perceptions.

(Continued)

KEY POINTS *(Continued)*

▌ Rumors and gossip are generated by black holes; regular communication prevents Bermuda Triangles and builds trust, relationships, loyalty, and involvement.

▌ Most leaders believe they communicate more than they do.

▌ Communication can improve employee retention.

▌ The 5:1 Feedback Ratio prevents Bermuda Triangles.

▌ Organizations run the risk of creating Bermuda Triangles with their customers when they neglect to communicate or to provide sufficient information; when there is a lack of information, customers fill in with the negative.

▌ Don't wait for concrete news to communicate with customers; let them know work is progressing.

▌ Don't leave it to the media to tell customers when there is a problem.

▌ Put yourself in your customer's shoes and look for potential Bermuda Triangles.

▌ Confirm orders, especially when transactions are paperless.

▌ Don't wait for completion of a project to give your customer updates.

▌ Let your customer know that you are working on solving their problems.

▌ Help your customer understand your working process: What is the next step, and the next step after that? What are the requirements for their participation in the process?

▌ Limit your use of jargon or technical language. When you do use it, define it.

4

BRAIN OPERATING PRINCIPLE 2:
Drive for Closure

People will strive for completion or a definitive answer, even when neither exists

"I need to make a decision right now. I can't live in limbo any longer," Anna proclaimed. *"I can't wait for three more weeks, until the company announces who is getting laid off, to decide whether or not I should move to Denver."*

So went the monologue of a coaching client, who found herself at the mercy of her OSE brain's Drive for Closure. The principle of Drive for Closure says that the OSE brain will strive for completion or a definitive answer—any answer—even when neither exists. The principle explains why the OSE brain will continue to look for answers until you give it different instructions: the OSE brain considers any open question a demand to find the answer.

Like Anna, if you've ever had a decision to make, lacked the necessary information or a clear direction, and felt an overwhelming urge to make the decision anyway, you've experienced the Drive for Closure. The OSE brain does not favor the experience of limbo, where there is no clear direction or ending, so it pushes toward the finish line. Even when you know you would be better off by waiting to make the decision or by taking the time to consider other information, you will still have the urge to close the question.

This principle of Drive for Closure explains why people find it so difficult to resist buying something immediately. Once you have felt the urge to acquire, you've put your brain in limbo, waiting for an answer. The limbo triggers your brain's Drive for Closure.

The need for closure is why goals motivate us. A goal is like a finish line for the brain, it directs the brain toward a particular end result, and provides a sense of satisfaction upon completion.

The Drive for Closure also explains why you feel the urge to finish an article in a magazine or just one more chapter in a book. It explains why some people read the ending of a novel before the beginning. It also explains why you are reluctant to leave even a lousy movie before the credits roll. People have a need for the answers that the ending of a story provides.

The late motivational theorist, David Berlyne, said that the Drive for Closure—while partially explained by several psychological theories—is rooted in the motivation of curiosity. In *The Story of Psychology*, author Morton Hunt talks about Berlyne's theory:

> *The drive to learn and understand, said Berlyne, could be accounted for in part by psychoanalytic theory, Gestalt psychology, and reinforcement theory, but a fuller explanation lies in the motivation of curiosity. In Berlyne's view, there is a subtler need behind curiosity than the desire for practical knowledge. Strange or puzzling situations arouse conflict in us, and it is the drive to reduce the conflict that impels us to seek answers. What motivated Einstein to develop his general theory of relativity was not its immense practical consequences but what he called a "passion for comprehension"—specifically, a need to understand why his special theory of relativity was at odds with certain principles of Newtonian physics. [Hunt, 1994, pp. 495-496]*

Berlyne noted that the Drive for Closure is not limited to important or urgent questions. He recognized the mental distress people feel when a question remains without an answer. Hunt quotes Berlyne's article, "A Theory of Human Curiosity," published in 1954: "Few phenomena have been the subject of more protracted discussion than human knowledge. Yet this discussion has usually paid little attention to the motivation underlying the quest for knowledge. . . . Strangely enough, many of the queries that inspire the most persistent searches for answers and the greatest cognitive distress when answers are not forthcoming are of no manifest practical value or urgency. One has only to consider some of the ontological inquiries of metaphysicians or the frenzy of crossword enthusiasts to be convinced of this." (Berlyne, 1954, pp. 180–191)

THE FINAL ANSWER

As Berlyne said, the Drive for Closure does not operate only when the answer to the question is of "practical value or urgency." For example, people feel and react to the Drive for Closure when a movie or other story has an ambiguous ending, even though there is no practical need to know or urgency attached. But, without an answer, the OSE brain continues to seek out closure by debating the possibilities. Everyone has at least some areas of their lives in which they aren't comfortable with the ambiguity of "we'll figure it out as we go along." The OSE brain has difficulty letting you have the wide, open space required to deal with ambiguity. The brain compels you to make a decision: "Is it this way or that way? Who has the right answer? Where is the logic?"

The degree of tolerance for ambiguity depends on your view of the importance of the issue or situation. The less invested you are, the faster and easier it is to let go of the need for closure. If you see a movie that has an ambiguous ending, you might puzzle over it for an hour or so, but forget about it by the time you go to sleep that night. However, if the ambiguity involves something more important than a movie ending, it's not so easy to give up on closure.

Remember the 2000 presidential election? The media were compelled to predict the winner, the candidates were compelled to declare victory, and the public was compelled to know the final answer. But, everyone had to wait over five weeks to get it.

During the evening and early morning hours following the closing of the polls on election day, the media made four different declarations about the result of the election. It was NBC who led the networks in first declaring Gore to be the winner of Florida at 8:00 P.M., effectively handing him the election. Two hours later, at 10:00 P.M., CNN changed the Florida results back to undecided, and the other networks soon followed. Around two o'clock in the morning, the Fox networks gave Bush the lead in Florida. Two hours later, the networks reversed their call again, pronouncing the election too close to call. NBC anchor Tom Brokaw admitted the media's embarrassment by saying, "We don't just have egg on our face—we have an omelet."

For several weeks following election night, there was a mass event of people living at the mercy of their brains' Drive for Closure. Not just the presidential candidates—Bush and Gore—or the media, but people all over the country wanted an answer and they wanted it now. Never mind that there was no rational reason why the recounts had to be completed quickly. Former secretary of state Warren Christopher, adviser to the Gore team, injected one of the few moments of sanity, when he said, "It's not as important to get it *right now* as it is to get it right."

Why did some people tolerate the open question of who would be the next president and others eagerly await the next news bulletin, hoping it would answer the question once and for all? Part of the difference had to do with the perceived importance of the question. Some people were indifferent to which candidate won the election and others had a strong bias.

The other part of the difference is that some people have a higher degree of tolerance for ambiguity than others, even when the uncertainty pertains to something important to them. The tolerance is either a natural characteristic of personality or a result of life experience. These people have the ability to live with open questions and to function well in situations without clear answers. They also have a difficult time empathizing with people who do not have a high tolerance for uncertainty.

FOR CRYING OUT LOUD, WHICH IS IT?

The principle of Drive for Closure is causing great difficulty in this new business environment, where people have to work with more ambiguity and more paradox. In the industrial economy, progress was linear and the rules of the game were well-defined. In this new world, progress is nonlinear and the rules of the game shift like sand underneath your feet. In the past, business answers were objective, and there was at least one person who knew the right answer, usually someone older or more experienced. Today, business answers are more subjective, and no one person has the right answer; in fact, in this new environment there can be many right answers and the challenge is in choosing among them.

What makes the frustration factor even greater is that in today's business world, not only are there many answers to choose from, but one answer often contradicts another. *Harvard Business Review* pinpointed this phenomenon, writing about the "cacophony of conflicting voices" in an editor's letter with a title that illustrates the frustration:

"For Crying Out Loud, Which Is It?" (Wetlaufer, 2000, p. 10) The editor likened the attempt to get straight answers about doing business in today's economy to the predicament of a skier who has taken a fall and is unable to get back upright. When that happens, other skiers gather around, offering advice and often contradicting one another. This invariably creates frustration for the fallen athlete, who just wants the one, right answer.

Like ambiguity, paradox—when a seemingly contradictory statement is true—sends the OSE brain into a determined search for proof of the one right answer. The brain will consider first one idea and then another. If one of the ideas seems more likely to be valid, you feel a natural inclination to pursue that idea, and look for further information that will support your conclusion. If you cannot identify a stronger case for one idea over another, you'll go back and forth, searching for some piece of evidence to point you in the right direction.

DRIVE AND STEREOTYPES

The Drive for Closure exacerbates people's natural tendency to categorize—often through stereotyping. Social psychologists define stereotypes as a "set of widely shared generalizations about the psychological characteristics of a group or class of people." (Reber, 1995, p. 754) Every person grows up with an entire atlas of stereotypes, which help your brain simplify the task of making sense of the world (see Chapter 6).

In *The Social Animal*, social psychologist Elliot Aronson points out that stereotyping is not "necessarily an intentional act of abuse; it is frequently merely a way we humans have of simplifying our view of the world, and we all do it." Aronson mentions an experiment by Patricia Devine, which "demonstrated that all of us are aware of the commonly held stereotypes associated with minorities. . . . Devine found that, under ordinary circumstances, those of us who are relatively unprejudiced can exert conscious vigilance that serves to prevent these stereotypes from popping into our minds and affecting our beliefs and behavior." (Aronson, 1998, pp. 308, 323)

Aronson explains that stereotyping is a form of attribution and that "in an ambiguous situation people tend to make attributions consistent with their beliefs or prejudices." (Aronson, 1998, p. 312)

Attribution theory, first developed by Fritz Heider, deals with the way people make inferences about the causes of human behavior—their own and others. Attribution theory has three basic assumptions: people attempt to determine the causes of behavior; people assign causes based on their experiences; and the attributed cause impacts the perceiver's own feelings and behavior.

When confronted with ambiguity, the Drive for Closure pushes people to close the question by making an attribution—which is basically an explanation or prediction—and the attribution may be part of a learned stereotype. For example, based on stereotypes, people once attributed certain characteristics to women that defined them as unfit for the business world. It was widely assumed that women were too emotional to make good business decisions; women were not as smart or as capable as men; women couldn't command the respect needed to run a business; and young women would get pregnant and leave their jobs to take care of children.

Although many changes have been made in society and in the business world, Aronson notes that these stereotypes about women survive even today.

> Have these changes impacted the stereotypes held of women? Not as much as one might imagine. In 1996, Janet Swim and Lawrence Sanna did a careful analysis of over 50 rather recent experiments on this topic and discovered that the results are remarkably consistent with those of the earlier experiments. Swim and Sanna found that, although the gender effects are not large, they are remarkably consistent: If a man was successful on a given task, observers tended to attribute his success to ability; if a woman was successful on that same task, observers tended to attribute her success to hard work. If a man failed on a given task, observers tended to attribute his failure either to bad luck or to lower effort; if a woman failed, observers felt the task was simply too hard for her ability level. [Aronson, 1998, p. 314]

The drive to categorize by stereotyping can hinder your ability to work effectively with other people, particularly in an environment where diversity is more and more prevalent. In this new environment, individuals often work in project teams with people of a different age, gender, race, background, culture, or education. When faced with the ambiguity of this diversity, your brain tries to simplify the task—closing the question by putting a label on each member of the team.

This rush to judgment can lead to false conclusions. And once the judgment is made, it is much more difficult to consider new information that might lead you to a different conclusion.

Stereotyping can make working relationships difficult because it can lead you to misunderstand someone's behavior, words, or motives. When you make attributions, assuming that you "know" someone because of a stereotype, you have set expectations about what they will do or say. Their actual behavior or words are seen as evidence of those expectations. However, their intentions may be completely different from how you read the situation. Your stereotypes keep you from seeing all the elements of a situation.

For example, let's say you have a stereotype that salespeople are always looking out for themselves, and one day a salesperson does something nice for you, like sending you a helpful book. Your stereotype will lead you to conclude that the salesperson is working from the ulterior motive of wanting to make you feel obligated to buy from them, when in fact, the salesperson may have sent the book out of a genuine desire to be helpful. If you react with suspicion and hostility, the salesperson may in turn make an assumption about you, and decide not to pursue the relationship. You may miss out on a working relationship that could have helped you be successful in your job.

Remember that attribution theory says that the inferences people make impact their own feelings and behavior. Therefore, stereotypes not only impact how you view another person, they also influence how you act toward that person. As Aronson says, stereotypes can be self-fulfilling prophecies: "When we hold erroneous beliefs or stereotypes about other people, our responses to them often cause them to behave in ways that validate those erroneous beliefs. . . . If people hold stereotypes of women as passive and dependent, or of blacks as lazy and stupid, they may treat them as such and inadvertently create the very behaviors or characteristics associated with these stereotypes. 'See,' they say to themselves, 'I was right all along about those people.'" (Aronson, 1998, p. 321)

Even though making attributions and stereotyping are natural processes of how people think, there are techniques you can use to prevent your stereotypes from pushing you into false conclusions. First, recognize when you are making inferences about someone else based on a stereotype. Second, check out your assumptions, by searching for information and evidence that contradict the stereotype, and not just for evidence that confirms your assumptions.

DRIVE FOR CLOSINGS

The Drive for Closure can be used for leading customers to favorable conclusions, for selling to a new customer, and for creating urgency to seal a deal. And its effectiveness is not limited to salespeople who are selling products. It can also be used to sell ideas.

Any good salesperson knows that leading a customer to draw their own conclusions is a better strategy than trying to tell them what to think. When you push a customer by attempting to force-feed them the answers, it can backfire, causing the customer to balk. We have been taught to be wary of salespeople and to expect them to give misleading information and answers just to make a sale. Instead of trying to push information, you can use the Drive for Closure to help the customer draw their own conclusions—conclusions that are favorable to your product or service.

How do you lead customers to draw their own conclusions? By posing questions that lead the customers closer and closer to your offering. To lead customers with questions, the questions need to be open questions, not closed (yes or no) questions.

One way to use questions to lead customers is to ask a question that gives the customer a choice between two alternatives: "Would you like it delivered on the fifth or the twelfth?" Sales guru Tom Hopkins calls this questioning technique "The Alternate Advance," which he defines as a "question that suggests two answers, both of which confirm that your prospect is going ahead." Hopkins says this technique works in a variety of situations, including booking an initial appointment. Hopkins suggests:

> . . . the professional never asks, "Could I come by this afternoon?"
>
> What answer does this suggest to most buyers? "No, I've really got a heavy schedule today. I'll call you when I have more time." Yes, he will. Sure.
>
> A professional gives two options: "Mr. Johnson, I'll be in your area this afternoon. Which would be more convenient, should I

stop by around two o'clock, or would you prefer that I wait until about three?"

When he says, "About three would be better," you have the appointment. You got it by suggesting two yeses instead of a no he would have jumped on. [Hopkins, 1982, p. 26]

Even if you are not a salesperson in the traditional sense, you can use this principle to sell your ideas by asking open questions that lead people to choose between alternatives. For example, let's say your competitor, XYZ Company, has just launched a new service and you want to launch a similar service with a pilot project, but you need to sell your colleagues on the idea. To lead your colleagues, you could start by asking them: "Have you heard about the new service XYZ Company is offering?" "What do you think about it?" "Have you heard any feedback from customers about the service?" "What do you think will be the biggest challenge in fulfilling the service?" Once you have the ball rolling, start to use Hopkins' "Alternate Advance" approach: "If we were to launch a similar service, do you think we should go all the way or test it out with a pilot project?" "Should we match XYZ's service or add our own features?" "Could we launch next quarter or should we plan for the quarter after?" The benefit to asking these types of questions is that once people start envisioning the service as part of your company, which the questions above help them do, it's not such a big leap to agree to the pilot project you are trying to sell.

Getting people to dip their toes in the water is a great strategy for selling (or persuading). Remember the concept of cognitive consistency? In the drive to appear consistent, once people make a public commitment, they will continue to make decisions that are consistent with that commitment. The more public the commitment, the more reluctant a person is to appear inconsistent. The drive to appear consistent can have extraordinary consequences. In his book, *Influence*, Robert Cialdini explains just how far people are willing to go to appear (or be) consistent:

Social scientists first became aware of its effectiveness in the mid-1960s when psychologists Jonathon Freedman and Scott Fraser published an astonishing set of data. They reported the results of an experiment in which a researcher, posing as a volunteer worker, had gone door to door in a residential California neighborhood making a preposterous request of homeowners. The homeowners were asked to allow a public-service billboard to be installed on their front lawns. To get an idea of just how the sign would look, they were shown a photograph depicting an attractive house, the view of which was almost completely obscured by a very large, poorly lettered sign reading DRIVE CAREFULLY. Although the request was normally and understandably refused by the great majority (83 percent) of the other residents in the area, this particular group of people reacted quite favorably. A full 76 percent of them offered the use of their front yards.

The prime reason for their startling compliance has to do with something that had happened to them about two weeks earlier: They had made a small commitment to driver safety. A different volunteer worker had come to their doors and asked them to accept and display a little three-inch-square sign that read BE A SAFE DRIVER. It was such a trifling request that nearly all of them had agreed to it. But the effect of that request was enormous. Because they had innocently complied with a trivial safe-driving request a couple of weeks before, these homeowners became remarkably willing to comply with another such request that was massive in size. [Cialdini, 1993, p. 72]

Cognitive consistency is the basis for the strategy of "getting your foot in the door." Once a customer has made a small agreement, such as a trial, a pilot, a taste test, or a small purchase, consistency means that they are more likely to make a bigger purchase.

A third method for using the Drive for Closure to make a sale is to create a sense of urgency about the opportunity. When you create urgency, people feel the need to close the question by making a decision. Quite often, that urgency will lead them to buy, right then, from you. The reason customers buy when you create urgency is that they are afraid they will lose the opportunity you have put before them. Psychological reactance theory, developed by psychologist Jack Brehm, explains why scarcity causes people to desire the scarce item. Brehm's theory is that people react against attempts to restrict or control their choices and decisions. The theory predicts that the more limited the availability of an object or activity, the more attractive it becomes. So, when you make customers believe that the opportunity will not be around at a later date, it becomes more appealing, and encourages customers to close the deal now.

THE FINISH LINE

The Drive for Closure is one of the reasons that it is difficult to walk away from a task without finishing it. It is why when you look at a To-Do list that has incomplete projects, you feel stressed. The status of incomplete is a difficult state for our brains to handle. Thus, the Drive for Closure is responsible for a big portion of the stress and mental fatigue that people feel on the job. The Drive for Closure is especially likely to cause stress when people feel like they are never accomplishing anything or when the end goal keeps changing. The constant ambiguity and inability to complete a project creates frustration, stress, and fatigue, not to mention a decline in productivity.

Martha Marshall works in government, and told me that recent changes in her agency, which processes disability claims, were causing immense frustration and stress for people. She wrote me that "The rules keep changing on a weekly—if not daily—basis with more and more documentation required, and no guidance as to when enough is enough." Because the system was not clear, the procedures were also unclear, which meant that people were wasting time redoing and revising paperwork. They were constantly guessing the correct process. One of Martha's colleagues said that even when she worked diligently for eight hours each day, it seemed like nothing was ever completed. She stated that in 25 years on the job, she had been frustrated many times, but she had never been so exhausted, discouraged, or burned out.

People can also feel Drive for Closure fatigue because of the blurred lines between work life and home life. Particularly today, with cell phones, pagers, laptops, portable e-mail, and even home offices, it is difficult to have mental closure at the end of a working day. The unresolved issues and unfinished tasks hang on and roll around in the mind, creating mental fatigue.

The following strategies can be used to create closure when you are involved with a long-term project or when you need to move from working on one project to another: First, break the project into small chunks of work. When you look at a big project as a series of smaller chunks, and you complete one of those chunks, the brain feels it has finished the task put in front of it. This strategy also works for situations when you need to move among projects. If you delineate a chunk of work to finish before you switch projects, your brain will have the closure it needs.

Another strategy that can be used to create closure is to develop a ritual to end your working day that signals your brain that work is done. You may already have one of these rituals. If you are in the habit of straightening up your desk and preparing it for work the next day, you have a ritual; if you check off the tasks you have completed and create a list of priorities for the next day, that can serve as a ritual, as well.

The important element of creating a closing ritual is that you pay attention when you are performing it. Don't let your mind wander into the territory of rehashing unresolved issues or creating anxiety over unfinished tasks. You will defeat the purpose of the closure ritual if you do not follow it through to the end.

CREATIVE DRIVE

Because the Drive for Closure is a result of the brain's search for meaning, it can be an indispensable tool in the right situation, like when it is used to solve problems and create ideas. To use the Drive for Closure to create ideas or solutions, ask a question, create a blank space, or lay out a series of clues, because when you ask a question or create a blank space, your Drive for Closure is triggered, and your OSE brain goes to work to try to find the answer or insight into a complex problem.

One of the fascinating uses of the Drive for Closure is to find links or relationships between a series of clues. Have you ever seen a movie or TV show where the detectives pin up the clues about a crime or series of crimes on a wall, so they can be viewed as one picture? That is an example of laying out clues for your Drive for Closure. When you lay out the clues and ask questions like, "What are the links here?" or "What do these have in common?" your brain will strive to find the answer. I use this technique with coaching clients who are searching for the right direction for their lives or careers. I help them create a map that captures their answers to a series of questions on one, big sheet of paper. Having it all on one big sheet of paper lets them see patterns and ideas.

The Drive for Closure is a great discovery tool, but it can also become a barrier when people let it operate too early in the problem-solving or creative process, when people insist on having the answer without taking time to consider if they are solving the right problem, or when they leap to analysis without spending sufficient time in creating alternatives.

This syndrome often happens in the brainstorming process. Before venturing very far into the difficult territory of creating possibilities, the tendency is to start evaluating those that are already on the table. Beginning the evaluation process too early shuts down the energy for creating new possibilities and closes the door to what can be the best solution. As many creativity veterans can testify, the most extraordinary ideas are often those that are voiced at that point in the session when it seems like the creative process has run out of steam. The last ideas are often the best ideas, because they connect and build on elements of the ideas that were raised earlier in the process.

Letting the Drive for Closure loose too early in a process can result in not solving the problem at all. Sometimes the urge to finish comes from the idea that the group has wasted too much time on the process already. Other times it is the result of wanting to get out of the discomfort of limbo. Either way, shutting down the creative process too early can short-circuit the ability to effectively solve the problem.

DRIVING PAST PROCRASTINATION

The principle of Drive for Closure is one of the most effective tools to enhance productivity by overcoming procrastination. Procrastination is a common malady among business people. It results in people wasting time, missing opportunities, underperforming, and suffering from high levels of stress.

People procrastinate because of many reasons. These reasons include:

I Fear of failure.

I Uncertainty about how to complete the task.

I Lack of skill or training.

I Feeling overwhelmed or intimidated.

I Perfectionism.

I Feeling overextended.

People procrastinate about starting projects, and about finishing them. There are two types of procrastinators: procrastinators who feel tension or fear; and those who are relaxed, who deny the importance of the work and focus on fun activities to distract themselves.

Sometimes a little procrastination can be helpful. It can give your brain time and space to think about something, to get a jump start on creation. It can also prevent you from wasting time on a project that is a priority one day and a moot point the next. However, for the most part, procrastination hinders our effectiveness at work—not to mention its impact on motivation and stress. Procrastination can waste time, energy, and resources. Studies show that 40 percent of people have experienced loss due to procrastination, and up to 25 percent of people report they have experienced chronic, debilitating procrastination. Those percentages add up to a substantial loss of productivity in the business world, not to mention the cost of the added stress.

There are two ways to use the principle of Drive for Closure to overcome procrastination. The first is to use Drive to start on a project, because once you start on a project, it is easier to continue. The second is to break a big, intimidating project into manageable chunks and use your Drive to start and finish them.

To break through procrastination, give your brain a small, specific goal, such as working on a project for a short period of time. I often use this technique (see The 15-Minute Bribe) to get started on something when I'd rather be doing something else.

ACTION TOOL: The 15-Minute Bribe

The 15-Minute Bribe helps you to start on a project when you are procrastinating. Begin by promising yourself that if you work on the project for just 15 minutes, you can turn your attention to something more pleasurable or less stressful.

Because of the Drive for Closure, once you start on a project, your brain strives for completion, so it is likely you will find yourself easily working longer than the 15 minutes you pledged. Using The 15-Minute Bribe, you can make significant inroads on your project. You may even surprise yourself and complete it.

The second technique for breaking through is useful when you are intimidated or overwhelmed by the size of a project. This technique involves dividing the project into smaller, manageable chunks and giving your brain the satisfaction of completing these smaller chunks (the same technique recommended earlier in "The Finish Line"). The chunks can be steps like making a list of tasks for the projects, organizing your notes and research materials into a folder or notebook, or drafting an outline.

You can also use this technique for an overwhelming list of e-mails or phone calls to return, or for a giant To-Do list. If answering all of your phone calls or e-mails is too intimidating, set yourself a goal to return just three messages now, and perhaps three more messages in the afternoon. Once your brain feels the satisfaction of a finish, the rest of those e-mails or calls will seem less overwhelming. If you have a giant To-Do list, choose a few priorities and circle them on the list. Tell your brain that these are the tasks that must be accomplished. When you finish them, you'll experience the satisfaction and energy boost of closure.

THE ORGANIZATIONAL DRIVE

When the principle of Drive for Closure operates in organizations, it affects business strategy, decision making, and innovation. The same Drive for Closure that pushes an individual to strive for completion or a definitive answer—even when neither exists—pushes organizations to do the same. When an organization succumbs to the collective Drive for Closure, it can influence business strategy and decision making by driving conclusions and assumptions. It can also squash innovation, when the urge for closure results in a controlling environment or one that discourages risk. On the other hand, thinking organizations can selectively use the principle to create the opportunity for experimentation and innovation by posing strategic questions, allowing for blank space, and by exploring multiple futures.

THE DRIVE FOR AN ANSWER

The principle of Drive for Closure is particularly relevant to businesses struggling to deal with the changes in this new environment, because ambiguity is a larger part of our everyday world, and answers aren't as clear-cut as they used to be. When cause and effect cannot be easily identified, choosing becomes more difficult, which makes developing the right strategy more difficult.

Take, for example, the ongoing development of the Internet and the business opportunities it offers. The brain—spurred by past business teachings that trained people to define, manage, and control—desperately wants to settle on an answer to the question of what the Internet is and will be, as if the final outcome is a certain station, where we will arrive on the train, disembark at that station, and the answer will be there, waiting for us. It's uncomfortable, difficult, and frustrating to not be able to predict what will happen, to have so much that is in doubt (ambiguous). Because of the discomfort, people tend to collectively jump at any answer that looks reasonable.

Here are just a few of the conclusions people jumped to in recent years:

I Everything will be electronic and paperless (no more documents, FedEx, catalogs, junk mail, etc.).

I Retail will die out and there will be ghost malls all over the country.

I People will no longer be necessary; everything will be automated.

I Business travel will no longer be necessary; business meetings will take place via videoconferencing or teleconferencing.

I Business success on the Internet will be solely based on eyeballs; no need for revenues or profits.

These conclusions are extreme. Just a few years of experience with the Internet economy demonstrated the fallacy of jumping to these types of extreme conclusions.

In the case of business strategy that involves the Internet, and other technology, problems arise when an organization lets the Drive for Closure compel it to choose a particular future too soon. Choosing one answer shuts down thinking about other potential futures, and when a group of people settle on one answer too early, it's easy to lose sight of indicators that the future is unfolding in a different way than they had planned.

Two dynamics operate in this situation: First, remember that once a decision is made, your brain tends to protect you from data that would cause cognitive dissonance, so your brain will filter out information that conflicts with what you chose to believe (see the chapter on the OSE brain for more on cognitive consistency and dissonance). Second, people are reluctant to admit that they made a wrong choice.

An organization that settles on one choice tends to filter out or discount information that is contrary to its decision. This kind of collective blind spot can jeopardize an entire business. One example of a company that chose the wrong future is Encyclopaedia Britannica. Weighted down by sunk costs (past investments) and the legacy of their sales force structure, executives at Encyclopaedia Britannica let the Drive for Closure push them to decide that a CD-ROM encyclopedia called Encarta could never compete with their product. The rationale for this decision was management's belief that Encarta was an inferior product to Britannica's own encyclopedia set when viewed from an academic perspective. Even from the standpoint of a word count—Encarta contained only seven million words, while a set of Britannica's contained 40 million—Encarta was inferior.

Britannica's direct sales force, which relied on commissions of $500 to $600 per sale, bolstered the decision to dismiss Encarta. Selling a CD-ROM could not possibly generate the kinds of commissions this sales force was accustomed to, so the group of people who were closest to Britannica's customers had no incentive to look beyond the flimsy rationale that an inferior product would never compete with the product sold by Encyclopaedia Britannica. Thus, a company with sales of $650 million dollars lost 80 percent of its sales in just five years and was eventually sold for less than half of its book value in 1996. A big price to pay for letting the Drive for Closure compel the organization to choose one right answer.

Instead of letting its Drive for Closure choose too early, Encyclopaedia Britannica could have experimented with an electronic version of its product that offered less information than the traditional set of books. The company could have created several scenarios to explore how computers might impact the marketplace. It could have even involved the sales reps in creating the scenarios and in problem solving.

EMBRACING PARADOX

The principle of Drive for Closure accounts for the need to have business strategy fit into the one right answer. In today's environment, pursuing more than one avenue—even when the two avenues conflict—can mean the difference between success and failure. Many people were taught to believe that there is one right way or one right choice. They were told to pick a direction and stick to it, or that when two options conflict, they could not pursue both. There are phrases that reinforce this idea, such as *singularity of purpose, you cannot be all things to all people,* and *you cannot have it both ways.*

In the classic book, *Built to Last,* Jim Collins and Jerry Porras pointed out that one of the characteristics of the successful companies they studied was the ability to embrace what Collins and Porras called "The Genius of the AND."

These successful companies do not limit themselves with the "Tyranny of the OR," defined as the "rational view that cannot easily accept paradox, that cannot live with two seemingly contradictory forces or ideas at the same time. The 'Tyranny of the OR' pushes people to believe that things must be either A OR B, but *not both.*" (Collins and Porras, 1994, p. 42)

Successful companies have embraced paradox by creating business strategies that do not require one right answer. Collins and Porras provide illustrations of companies that have succeeded by pursuing seemingly contradictory strategies: these illustrations include companies that believe they can be driven both by values AND by profit; companies that can seek to do well in the short term AND in the long term; and companies that can have both a clear vision and sense of direction, AND the ability to experiment with new possibilities. In each of these cases, not settling for one right way seems contradictory to the prevailing wisdom of business. (Collins and Porras, 1994, p. 43)

Having to sacrifice company values to make a profit, for example, is an accepted assumption in business. However, Merck & Company has succeeded by ignoring the drive for one right answer, and pursuing seemingly contradictory strategies: Merck is driven both by values and by profit. Collins and Porras explain Merck's viewpoint with a quote by George Merck II from a speech he gave to the Medical College of Virginia in the 1950s: "We try to remember that medicine is for the patient. It is not for the profits. The profits follow, and if we have remembered that, they have never failed to appear." Merck has demonstrated this philosophy at a number of key points in the history of the company, even going so far as to give away a drug that cured river blindness to patients in third-world countries who couldn't afford the drug. (Collins and Porras, 1994, p. 48)

Merck isn't a not-for-profit organization. It does seek to provide a return on investment for shareholders, and profits the company can use to fund research and development. However, it does not sacrifice its value of "medicine for the patient" for the singular purpose of making a profit. Unfortunately, few companies have this kind of blended vision. When you combine the lesson that profits should come first with the need for choosing one right answer, it is difficult for most business people to fathom "The Genius of the AND."

DRIVE FOR CONTROL

Drive for Closure also affects a company's strategic thinking when the need for closure causes an organization to place a high emphasis on control. This emphasis impacts strategy because it compels organizations to resist or discount ambiguous factors in the competitive environment. When the Drive for Closure runs rampant in an organization's culture, it creates an environment where control is overemphasized. In a control-based culture, actions that involve ambiguity, such as taking risks, experimenting, investing for the long term, or investing in projects that are not easily quantifiable are all frowned upon.

One of the reasons that established companies resist investing in Web-based business practices is that the ambiguity conflicts with their overemphasis on control. When an established company analyzes the payback from Web-based business practices in relationship to their current business model, the analysis shows a return on investment that is intangible, tenuous, and long term, all of which add up to an investment that control-oriented companies are reluctant to make. In a control-oriented company, preference is given to those investments that show an immediate financial return that is tightly linked (in a cause-and-effect relationship) to the investment.

To make the Internet investment even less attractive, these companies are confronted with the loss of control that is inherent in doing business over the Internet. These losses include:

I **Loss of control over customers', suppliers', and competitors' access to information.**

I **The increased potential for customers to share information and opinions about the company with each other.**

I **Reduced control over information about prices, which prevents companies from setting prices differently for different customers or in different geographies.**

In addition to discounting ambiguous trends, like the Internet, organizations that focus on control may also discount nontraditional competitors, which can lead to a significant loss of market share. When the business environment shifts, the factors used to evaluate competition often shift as well, but companies that are focused on controlling their environment are reluctant to broaden their viewpoint to the point that they can acknowledge that shift. Meanwhile, their nontraditional competitors are stealing away their customers, their revenues, and their future.

For example, Compaq made the mistake of discounting Dell Computer as a legitimate competitor, during the days when Dell was growing from its original incarnation of PC's Limited to what is known today as Dell Computer. Patrick Dryden, an analyst for the Giga Information Group who was formerly a reporter, told a story in the May 1999 issue of *Worth* magazine about Compaq's dismissal of Dell. Dryden was interviewing Rod Canion, one of Compaq's founders, and asked about Dell. According to Dryden, "Canion sneered and referred to PC's Limited as a novelty that wouldn't last." (Cringely, 1999, p. 108) Just ten years later, Dell was a close second to Compaq in PC sales and had surpassed Compaq in corporate-desktop PC sales.

DRIVE FOR DECISIONS

The problematic effects of the Drive for Closure are not limited to strategic questions. They can also be detected in other decision-making and problem-solving situations.

Today's economy of fast business triggers the organizational Drive for Closure and can compel an organization to make hasty decisions. In fact, a survey of 479 managers and 339 workers conducted by Kepner-Tregoe, Inc. showed that 77 percent of managers and 65 percent of workers felt that the number of decisions they were expected to make during a typical workday had increased. The majority of managers and workers also said the average amount of time they were given to make each decision either decreased or stayed the same.

When a company sees changes taking place in its business environment, it feels the pressure to make changes in its business. The pressure can lead to making decisions without considering all of the ramifications to the organization, its products, and its customers.

Entrepreneur Norm Brodsky, a veteran of six businesses, described his experience with Drive for Closure in one of his *Inc.* magazine columns, "Hurry Up and Wait." Brodsky was trying to decide whether or not to acquire a competitor that was available for a good price. Acquiring the company would help him meet a driving passion for having a company that registered over $100 million in sales. However, there were good reasons not to buy the company, because it had major financial problems. Not wanting to miss out on the opportunity to acquire the company, Brodsky downplayed the problems and focused on the $100 million goal. Brodsky confessed, "It was a bad deal. In my heart, I *knew* it was a bad deal. From a business standpoint, there was no justification for doing the acquisition. . . . But you don't listen to your inner voice when you're being driven by a sense of urgency. You override your good instincts. You make excuses. You tell yourself what you want to hear. I'd turned around other insolvent companies before. . . . So I went ahead and bought the company. Fourteen months later we filed for protection from creditors under Chapter 11." (Brodsky, 1998, p. 27)

When you feel this kind of drive to make a decision, discipline yourself to argue both or all sides of the issue convincingly. In the example above, Brodsky recognized the negatives of the deal, but he brushed over the problems. If he had taken the time to argue the cons as convincingly as the pros, he might have passed on the acquisition opportunity.

Arguing more than one side of an issue is difficult because of the tendency to choose the one, right answer and close the question. In early years as students, we were taught the elements of debate—to choose an opinion and create a logical argument for that opinion. We were not taught to dialogue, which focuses more on discussion instead of on who is right or wrong.

The technique of arguing more than one side can also be used when one person on a team is pushing hard for one, particular answer (at the mercy of their Drive for Closure) and causing conflict and problems in the process. If that person is given the assignment to construct a feasible argument for a different answer, it opens up the opportunity for a more effective discussion of the issue.

This technique can also be used when two team members are doggedly sticking to their opinions without listening to other possibilities, and creating a stalemate on a project. Challenge each of them to construct a valid argument for their opposition's point of view.

The principle of Drive for Closure also plays a role in companies solving the wrong problem. For example, the corporate drive may push an organization to pinpoint the reasons that something failed, instead of asking how to prevent a similar situation or what can be learned from the failure. The corporate drive can push an organization to identify the person at fault—someone they can point the finger at—instead of looking for the bigger reasons why. This drive can also push an organization to stop investigating a problem too soon, when investigation does not continue beyond the first logical answer to the origins of the problem; all of these results occur because of the urge to close the question.

SILVER BULLETS

The Drive for Closure is also the culprit in the corporate tendency to look for a silver bullet resolution to a problem or situation. The silver bullet got its name from the 1930s belief that supernatural beings—like werewolves—could be killed with a silver bullet. The phrase *silver bullet* is used in business to refer to solutions that seem almost magical, in that they appear to be quick resolutions to difficult problems.

The compelling drive to have closure on a situation makes the silver-bullet solution very appealing, because it seems to offer a simple, one-time fix for the problem. However, a silver-bullet solution can end up being a mirage. Upon close examination, which usually happens once an organization starts implementation, the mirage begins to fall apart or it disappears completely.

The Drive for Closure makes businesses vulnerable to advice, trends, and fads that appear to provide silver-bullet solutions. The reengineering fad is a good example of a fad that appeared to be a silver-bullet solution. Reengineering (also known as business process reengineering) was the big management fad of the early 1990s. It involved breaking an organization down into component parts and then putting it back together again to create a new machine. In this fad, process was all-important, and people were pegs to slot into the holes in the process—hence reengineering became synonymous with downsizing, when thousands of people lost their jobs in reengineered businesses.

As a silver-bullet solution, reengineering was alluring to businesses because it made promises about increasing productivity and competitiveness, as well as lowering costs and defects. It also meshed with the prevailing Taylor-influenced management style that condoned ignoring the human side of the business. However, whether it was a fault in the technique itself or a failure in implementation (as the founders of reengineering claim), for many companies, reengineering turned out badly. In 1994, a survey by Arthur D. Little showed that only 16 percent of managers using reengineering were fully satisfied and 68 percent were encountering unexpected problems. Not long after, even the creators of reengineering, Michael Hammer and James Champy, said publicly that many attempts at reengineering were falling short of their goals.

Some of the other silver-bullet solutions of recent years include management by objectives, intrapreneurship, managerial grid, excellence, management by walking around, quality circles, zero inventory, empowerment, visions, portfolio theory, and the balanced scorecard. None of these trends, ideas, or fads are necessarily useless or harmful, but neither are any of them the one, final solution that business hoped they would be. Perhaps the business world is inching toward the understanding that there is no one formula that applies to everyone and every situation.

DRIVING INNOVATION

The Drive for Closure can either shut down innovation or be used to encourage it. Organizations that give in to a strong need for control are likely to shut down innovation. Those that resist the need for control and instead encourage exploration and experimentation are rewarded by lucrative innovation. Control demands certainty and certainty is the opposite of experimentation. When the culture of an organization is built on control and certainty, it creates an environment where innovation cannot survive.

Control-based organizations tend to study the problem, perform research and analyses, develop alternatives, test the alternatives, create a plan, and then run the plan through an approval process before taking action. This process ignores anything that smacks of ambiguity, change, or nonlinearity. And today's business environment is chock full of ambiguity, change, and nonlinearity.

Control-based organizations are more likely to develop incremental products and services in literal, verbatim response to what customers say they want, instead of investing in innovation that would give them a true competitive advantage. They tend to be comfortable with strategies that address today's customer issues, but not tomorrow's. Control-based organizations require proof that a product has a sizeable market before even exploring its development. Unfortunately for these companies, many innovative products require time in the marketplace before customers actually see the benefits and incorporate them into their work in a way that proves out a sizeable market.

Ideas and input in meetings can be shut down by the Drive for Closure. The scene often plays out like this: the boss lays out his understanding of a problem and his ideas about how to resolve the problem, thinking that this will jump start a discussion of the problem and the brainstorming of ideas to solve it. Instead, because of the Drive for Closure and the positional power that is derived from the boss' leadership role, the resulting discussion turns into more of a drive to prove the boss right than an exploration of possible solutions.

Business people who want to encourage ideas and input from

their colleagues and subordinates need to curb their own drive to provide the answers, using questions to draw out the ideas and input of others. In an interview with the *Harvard Business Review*, George Conrades, chairman and CEO of Akamai, talked about his role in the discussions the management team has about the key challenges facing the company. Conrades is a good example of a leader who knows how to encourage input from employees. "My role is to be the referee in those discussions. I'm an active participant in them, but I'm also the guy who steps back from the fray, synthesizes everything that's been said, and makes sure the argument's moving forward rather than in a circle. I might jump up to the white board, for instance, to capture the key ideas and force people to focus on them. I'm also the guy who says, 'Enough.' When it is clear we've gone as deep as we're going to go, I stop the debate, and we finalize the decision. I'm careful to never play that role in an authoritarian, top-down way. There are a lot of very, very smart people in this company, with IQs a lot higher than mine. The last thing I'd want to do is shut them up." (Carr, 2000, p. 122)

The Drive for Closure can be used strategically by organizations to encourage innovation. This happens when an organization asks questions that encourage exploration and experimentation, and when it allows people the time and space to explore and create. When the leadership of an organization asks questions that encourage exploration and experimentation, they create an environment where the Drive for Closure is used to find new possibilities, instead of closing them off. Remember that questions send your brain on a search for answers. Asking questions encourages people to find examples that can serve as creative fodder or to consider the situation from a different perspective.

Organizations also put the Drive for Closure to work for them when they create a blank space for exploration. At 3M, managers have adopted the now legendary 15 percent rule: 3M employees can devote up to 15 percent of their time to projects of their own choosing, without seeking approval from above or even bothering to tell managers what it is they are working on. This rule, in essence, creates a blank space, an opportunity for innovation and new ideas, as the Drive for Closure rushes to fill the blank space. Unfortunately, the typical machine-based metaphor that rules business seeks to ensure that people are scheduled up to their capacity. But, when every hour of a person's time is spoken for, there's no space to think about and create new ideas.

EXPLORATORY DRIVE

Organizations can prevent the negative consequences of the Drive for Closure by deciding to explore several possibilities at once. It's not the easiest thing to do, but it is becoming an essential skill in this ambiguous, paradoxical environment.

One way to explore several possibilities is to use scenario thinking to envision how different factors could affect the way the future unfolds. Scenarios are basically what-if stories that explore potential futures for a product, a business, or an industry. Scenarios consider the most relevant and pressing external forces, certain or uncertain, that the business or industry is likely to encounter in the future.

Scenario thinking helps companies anticipate radical changes in their industry and see opportunities in those changes. For instance, developing scenarios helped Royal Dutch/Shell anticipate the fall of Communism in Russia and its effect on natural gas prices. Playing out scenarios gave Pacific Gas & Electric insights for better plans to take care of customers in the aftermath of California earthquakes. Developing and learning from scenarios has also helped numerous companies spot new customer needs and markets.

Peter Schwartz, president of the Global Business Network, popularized the use of scenarios in business planning. Schwartz learned about using scenarios as a futurist at SRI International, and later in working with Pierre Wack and Arie de Geus of Royal Dutch/Shell. In his book, *The Art of the Long View*, Schwartz explained the advantages of using scenarios: "Thinking through these stories, and talking in depth about their implications, brings each person's unspoken assumptions about the future to the surface. Scenarios are thus the most powerful vehicles I know for challenging our 'mental models' about the world, and lifting the 'blinders' that limit our creativity and resourcefulness." (Schwartz, 1996, p. xv) In addition to the advantages Schwartz described, scenario thinking helps to appease the Drive for Closure because it provides a sense of closure for several possibilities at once. If you would like more information on using scenario thinking to pacify your Drive for Closure, I highly recommend *The Art of the Long View* by Peter Schwartz (the paperback edition has an excellent user's guide).

KEY POINTS

I The OSE brain will strive for completion or a definitive answer, even when neither exists.

I The OSE brain does not like limbo.

I The Drive for Closure is why goals motivate people.

I The Drive for Closure is not limited to important or urgent questions.

I When confronted with ambiguity, people feel the need for resolution one way or another.

I When confronted with ambiguity about another person, the Drive for Closure pushes people to close the question by making an attribution—which is basically an explanation or prediction—and the attribution may be part of a learned stereotype.

I Stereotypes hinder people's ability to work effectively with other people.

I Use the Drive for Closure to sell customers by leading them with questions, by getting them to agree to a trial, and by creating a sense of urgency.

I Incomplete projects cause stress.

I The Drive for Closure can be used to solve problems and generate ideas.

I You can use Drive for Closure to break through procrastination by setting small, specific goals or breaking projects into chunks of work.

I The Drive for Closure pushes organizations to jump to conclusions.

I Successful organizations embrace paradox by using the "Genius of the AND" instead of being at the mercy of the "Tyranny of the OR."

I Overemphasis on control results in missed opportunities, discounting ambiguous trends, and shutting down innovation.

I The Drive for Closure can lead to hasty decisions; learn to argue both sides.

I Organizations have a tendency to look for silver-bullet solutions, making businesses vulnerable to bad advice, fads, and trends.

I Encourage innovation by asking questions and creating a blank space for exploration.

I Scenario thinking can appease the Drive for Closure.

5

BRAIN OPERATING PRINCIPLE 3: Infinite Loop Thinking

When people are stuck in a thinking loop, they are unable to see alternatives

"What if I lose my job? I won't be able to make my house payment or my car payment. Without a car, I won't be able to look for a new job. In this economy, I'll never find a good job anyway. I'll have to go on unemployment or get a job in a fast food restaurant. Then I'll be stuck in a minimum wage job forever. Who will hire me when they find out I was laid off and had to take a minimum wage job? Where will I live on minimum wage, anyway? I'll have to move back in with my parents. What if I lose my job?"

When you're stuck in Infinite Loop Thinking, your brain goes over and over a problem or situation, always arriving back at the same original problem. Even if you add steps to the loop during some repetitions, you invariably arrive back at the same point. The principle of Infinite Loop Thinking says that when people are stuck in a thinking loop—usually when they are obsessed with a problem or situation—they are unable to see alternatives.

Infinite Loop Thinking is named after the computer programming term: infinite loop. When I was learning basic computer programming in college, the worst sin you could commit was to create an infinite loop in your program, because an infinite loop would order the computer to perform the same series of steps over and over and over, tying up the mainframe computer indefinitely until the loop was discovered and snipped.

Infinite Loop Thinking, like a computer programming infinite loop, can tie up your brain until you're able to break the cycle. Some loops are easily identified, while others are more difficult to see, and more complex.

WORRY LOOPS

Infinite Loop Thinking that is emotionally charged is often referred to as *awfulizing*. Awfulizing happens when a person is stuck seeing only the awful possibilities of a situation and continuing to dwell on the worst possible consequences. Awfulizing is a particularly difficult Infinite Loop to snip, because such strong emotions are involved. Even if the person is introduced to possibilities that are positive and have a good chance of happening, their OSE brain will continue to run the awfulizing Infinite Loop.

Worry loops and awfulizing are built on faulty assumptions woven in among valid conclusions. The assumptions are faulty because, although they are possible, they are also improbable and usually blown way out of proportion. What creates the loop is that each step in the loop is dependent on the previous step becoming true. So, in the preceding example, not being able to make the car payment is dependent on losing your job, and not having a car is dependent on not making the car payment, and so on. When people are stuck in this kind of loop, they cannot see that the steps in the loop have a low probability of occurrence, and it is difficult for them to see alternatives as legitimate possibilities.

Some people have built a core competency in worrying. They are able to trigger an Infinite Loop with minor provocation. If even a small problem appears, they start readying themselves for the worst-case scenario. Fear (appearing in the guise of worry) soon creates an Infinite Loop of disaster.

With champion worriers, the Infinite Loop starts with a few negative thoughts. Then, they begin imagining extremely negative consequences. They won't just make a mistake, they'll make a whopper. They won't just fall a little behind on their bills, they'll be bankrupt. When a champion worrier is caught in the grip of catastrophic thoughts, they lose perspective on the reality of the situation. The fact that their loop is based on extremes might be obvious to other people,

---

ACTION TOOL: Get Off the Merry-Go-Round

The Get Off the Merry-Go-Round action tool helps you identify the danger signals of an Infinite Loop, and recommends three strategies to break out of Infinite Loop Thinking.

You're in danger of an Infinite Loop if:

- You want to solve a problem, but don't have the information and don't want to wait to get it.
- You are emotionally entangled.
- You are feeling overwhelmed.
- Someone says you are not facing the facts.
- You are stuck in linear thinking.
- You do not have emotional closure on a situation, issue, or problem.

Strategies for snipping an Infinite Loop:

1. Map it: Write down each step in your thinking loop. Identify at what point your reasoning becomes circular.
2. Use "Who says?" to identify faulty assumptions. If you're thinking, "I'll never find another job like this one," ask yourself "Who says?"
3. Limit your worrying. Decide to think about your worries only during specified times and for a set time period. For example, you might decide to worry only from 11:00 A.M. to 11:10 A.M. and from 7:00 P.M. to 7:10 P.M. If you find yourself in a worry loop at another time during the day, stop and tell yourself "I'll worry about that at 7."

---

but each step in the loop makes perfect sense to the worrier. In a worry loop, a simple situation becomes do-or-die, as the circumstances and their consequences become exaggerated.

INFINITELY RIGHT

People think they are right more than they are. In fact, in about 15 percent of the instances in which individuals are absolutely positive that they are right, they are actually wrong. This overconfidence bias was proven by three researchers: Baruch Fischhoff, Paul Slovic, and Sarah Lichtenstein. The researchers also showed that the discrepancy between correctness of response and overconfidence increases when the respondent is more knowledgeable—the more knowledgeable people are, the more overconfident they tend to be.

How do you know when you are in the Infinite Loop of needing to be right? When you hold on to your position, and do not consider the possibility that there might be another viewpoint or option, you are likely stuck in an Infinite Loop. The more right you think you are, the more you stick to your beliefs, the more right you think you are.

Part of the reason for the reinforcing loop is that if you consider the possibility that you might be wrong, you experience cognitive dissonance. Remember that cognitive dissonance is a state of mental tension or discomfort caused by trying to hold two conflicting beliefs at the same time. Your brain doesn't like this discomfort, so it searches for reinforcement and reasons why the belief you're clinging to is the correct one and why the conflicting idea is wrong.

INFINITE LOOP OF PERFECTION

Perfectionistic thinking can also trigger an Infinite Loop. Perfectionistic thinking is the belief that something has to be perfect. It can trigger an Infinite Loop because it focuses on extremes—the extremes of needing to do something perfectly or all the way.

Two of my clients found themselves paralyzed by a perfectionistic Infinite Loop. Cheryl and Alan sat at the conference table, with calendars, file folders, and piles of Post-it Notes. They both looked in despair at the jumble of tasks, overwhelmed by the sheer volume of the projects clamoring for their attention. Earlier in the day, the two business partners and I had a conversation about their business. They were both experiencing high levels of stress and worrying about the business. As they talked, I started to hear symptoms of the loop. Cheryl and Alan were stuck in an Infinite Loop based on two faulty assumptions: (1) With so much to do, they didn't have time to plan; and (2) The two partners could get more done in the time available than any two human beings could possibly accomplish. When I explained the dynamic of Infinite Loop Thinking, they recognized that even though they thought they didn't have time to plan and prioritize, they would continue to be stuck in their thinking loop until they laid out these projects and made some realistic choices among priorities.

The three of us spent several hours identifying key projects and priorities and using Post-it Notes to create a timeline—placing, moving, and swapping project tasks. The most difficult part of creating the timeline was making tradeoffs among priorities. The perfectionist assumption about priorities—that Cheryl and Alan should be able to accomplish an overwhelming number of projects in an unrealistic time frame—was part of what had thrown them into Infinite Loop Thinking. At first, as we posted project steps, most of the work went into a few short weeks. But once the two partners saw the work laid out against the actual days and dates in black and white, they realized how unrealistic their thinking about priorities had become. With the projects spelled out in a workable timeline, the two partners were able to snip their Infinite Loop.

I see the perfectionist Infinite Loop often in clients who will not take even a small step toward their goal because they think they shouldn't do anything if they cannot do it all the way (perfectly). It's particularly evident when it comes to marketing plans. Clients often feel that if they cannot implement the whole marketing program, they shouldn't do anything. In other words, if they cannot produce a comprehensive, impressive package, they shouldn't do any marketing until they can, or, if they cannot send information to a big group of people, they should wait to send information to anyone.

The need to be perfect can produce a paralysis that is caused by the fear of not being good enough. It can keep people from starting a project and it can also keep them from finishing one. Fortunately, perfectionist Infinite Loops are one of the easiest Infinite Loops to break. The trick is to convince yourself to take a few small steps. You don't have to give up believing in your Infinite Loop if you just agree to take those small steps.

THE LOOP AND THE RUT

Question: What is the difference between a rut and a groove? Answer: Depth perception.

Infinite Loop Thinking is not limited to problem situations. It also occurs when people think about an idea in the same way, over and over. So, an Infinite Loop is a thinking rut.

There is nothing wrong with thinking about an idea over and over. It's often the key to solving a problem. The difficulty arises when you repeatedly think about an idea in the same way, without trying out new possibilities or pathways. It's like walking the same circular path every day without ever trying out one of the branches of the path. You see the same sights over and over. And without any change in the stimuli, you are unlikely to change your thinking or to generate new ideas.

Einstein was talking about Infinite Loop Thinking when he said you cannot solve a problem with the same thinking that created it. Einstein was referring to the idea that solving a problem often requires looking at a situation in a completely, different way. It's natural when solving problems to look to what has worked in the past. Unfortunately, when people stick only to what they know, they miss out on other possibilities—possibilities that may hold the answer to the problem.

An Infinite Loop rut also occurs when someone makes the same mistake over and over, when they do not recognize that they are stuck in the same circumstances and making the same (bad) decision they have made in the past. When a person is in an Infinite Loop rut, they often operate on autopilot, reacting in the same way they have reacted previously.

CAREER LOOPS

In my coaching work, I see people who are stuck in Infinite Loops about their careers. Even if they are miserable in their jobs, they are reluctant to diverge out of thinking, "I need this job to pay my bills . . . I'm not qualified to do anything else . . . There are only a few companies in this area where I could do this type of work . . . My company is the highest paying in the area . . . I need the security of a large company . . . I need this job to pay my bills." If I question these people about their dependence on a particular job, I can usually trigger them to run through their loop simply by asking why.

Part of this loop can be attributed to the old, industrial-economy assumptions about careers. In the past:

I Changing jobs rarely involved changing careers.

I If a resume included more than a couple of job changes that involved switching companies, a person was viewed as a job-hopper, someone who either could not or would not stick with a job.

I People who left one career to pursue another after investing years in a certain area were few and far between.

I In the old environment, careers were slotted into a limited number of boxes. If it did not have a specific title, a description, a college major, pay ranges, and a governmental identification code, it was not a real career.

In today's environment, these assumptions have been turned up-side down:

I Job changes often involve company and even industry changes.

I Frequent job changes are viewed as an asset rather than a liability.

I People have more latitude to change careers.

I Brand new careers are born every day as new industries are started.

I Because of the talent shortage, companies are more willing to give someone a shot at doing something new.

Sometimes the Infinite Loop about career is based on the investment people have made in a particular company or career. They feel that changing jobs or changing careers will render the time and energy they have already invested a waste. Instead of seeing how their experiences can be incorporated into a new opportunity and benefit them in that new arena, they remain stuck in the loop of "What about all the years I've invested in my education and my experience in this particular job?"

It is very natural to feel this way, since the old idea of success was based on climbing up a ladder. Even if a person hated the work, or the ladder was against the wrong wall, they still felt they were succeeding if they were proceeding in a linear fashion, one step above the other. Each of those steps were measured by increases in status and pay. Many people in today's world haven't made the transition to the new success model, which is based on the experiences you have and the expertise and ideas you can offer, rather than on linear progression. Today, status and pay are important, but they are not the sole measure of success, as they used to be.

ORGANIZATIONAL INFINITE LOOPS

Once upon a time there was a group of managers who were industriously slashing and chopping a swath through a dense forest. The group had been hard at work for a long time when suddenly they heard a faint message from above—words that sounded like, "*Wrong forest.*" Since the message was faint and difficult to decipher, the group of managers ignored the words and continued their work. Time passed and soon the managers once again heard the faint message from above, "*Wrong forest.*" Again the group of managers refused to listen. Once more, time passed until the managers heard the message again from above, this time louder and more distinct, "*You're in the wrong forest!*" The group of managers conferred, debating the validity of the message. As a group, they decided that the messenger must be misguided, so they hollered back, "*Shut up, we're making progress!*"

As the preceding story illustrates, organizations are not immune to Infinite Loop Thinking, which can blind them to marketplace realities. They can get stuck in Infinite Loops about their customers, marketplace, or organizational capabilities, and lose sight of what is actually happening outside the loop.

Organizations that have been very successful for a period of time are especially prone to creating Infinite Loops that blind them to changes. It's easy to fall into a familiar and comfortable thinking pattern, but it can be very dangerous in today's environment. When organizations are stuck in a circular thinking pattern, they fail to look outside their comfort zone to see the changes happening in the business marketplace; they fail to take new competitors seriously; and, they fail to make the necessary changes to stay competitive.

GROUPTHINK LOOPS

The phenomenon of groupthink is one example of an Infinite Loop shared by a group of people. Groupthink occurs when a group develops its own subculture and viewpoint, and in the process of reinforcing that subculture and viewpoint, becomes deaf and blind to outsiders and alternatives.

Social psychologist Irving Janis studied group behavior, communication, and decision making. Based on his research, Janis developed the theory of groupthink, which he published in the 1960s. Janis defines groupthink as "a deterioration of mental efficiency, reality testing, and moral judgment that results from in-group pressures." (Janis, 1967, p. 9) Every group, no matter how large or how small, develops rules and norms that guide behavior and the thoughts and attitudes of the group's members. For individual members, the decision to conform to the group depends on their viewpoint. If the group itself and continued membership in it is important to the individual, he or she is likely to conform.

Infinite Loops of groupthink are created when group members take conforming to extremes. For example, loops of groupthink are created and reinforced when the group limits incoming information to that which conforms to their shared beliefs or to the majority viewpoint. When a group creates a loop, and most of their conversations are with each other, they reinforce their shared opinions and ideas, and ignore any conflicting ideas that may surface. In fact, their brains help them screen out conflicting information. As you will recall, when your brain tries to hold two conflicting beliefs at the same time, cognitive dissonance occurs, which is uncomfortable. Because of the discomfort, the brain will try to reduce dissonance by discounting one belief in favor of another, or sometimes by screening out information that does not support the chosen belief. For people who have chosen allegiance to a particular group, they will not only discount conflicting information, they may become deaf or blind to ideas that disagree with the group's. When groupthink is at its strongest, if a person within the group does dare to question or to express doubts, the dissenter is labeled as disloyal or not a team player. Creating an Infinite Loop is like building a bubble around the group—criticism is repelled, while inside the bubble the group is certain that they are right and everyone else is either ignorant or just plain wrong.

A group is in particular danger of developing a groupthink loop if it is homogenous. Homogenous groups tend to have similar experiences, to share similar beliefs, and to see situations and problems in a particular way. These similarities, which make it easier for homogenous groups to work together, also create group blindness to alternative possibilities.

Social psychologists, including Janis, have used the theory of groupthink to explain the decisions made during a number of political events, such as the Bay of Pigs invasion, the Korean War, Pearl Harbor, the escalation of the Vietnam war, the Third Reich, the Watergate cover-up, and the explosion of the space shuttle *Challenger*. The *Challenger* disaster, which happened in 1986, is a vivid example of how groupthink can cause people to ignore important information. The *Challenger* disaster is particularly memorable because of the shuttle's historic passenger—the first civilian, teacher Christa McAuliffe. McAuliffe was to teach science lessons from space, so many of the nation's schoolchildren were watching when the shuttle exploded just seconds after liftoff.

Investigations after the catastrophe revealed that defective O-rings at the joints of the solid rocket boosters were the cause of the explosion, and that engineers had warned executives at Morton Thiokol (the maker of the solid rocket boosters) about potential problems. But the executives didn't take the engineers' warnings seriously, and they downplayed the problems in discussions with NASA administrators. To add to the problem, NASA administrators were focused on the need to launch because of the political ramifications for future funding and the "teacher-in-space" program if the launch did not happen. Together, the Morton Thiokol executives and NASA administrators were caught in an Infinite Loop of groupthink. In a meeting the night before the disastrous launch, they turned on their blinders and convinced each other that the engineers were overreacting.

The *Challenger* catastrophe is just one example of how people conform to the group's viewpoint, causing groupthink. There are a number of studies that show the tendency to conform in groups. The most famous studies were performed by Solomon Asch during the 1950s. Asch demonstrated that people find it difficult to disagree with a majority viewpoint. According to Asch's studies, in situations where the majority of a group publicly supported the wrong answer to a question, about 37 percent of people conformed to the majority by giving the wrong answer even when they knew it was wrong. Asch's studies show how groupthink can persist, because people are reluctant to openly disagree with the majority viewpoint.

People are more likely to conform to the group in situations of ambiguity and uncertainty. Since today's environment is more uncertain and ambiguous, there is more danger that people will conform to groups and groupthink.

The major drawback of groupthink for an organization is that the whole of the group ends up being less than the sum of its parts. A groupthink loop limits the ability of the group members to think in different ways. The group has less brainpower than if each member were thinking independently. Also, when groupthink is at work, creativity and innovation are channeled into very limited avenues that are acceptable within the group's norms. Finally, when groupthink is operating, people in the organization become blind to shifts and changes in the marketplace.

INFINITE BLINDERS

The effects of Infinite Loop Thinking are evident in a number of those who hold positions of power. When those in power act as though they are always right, they are invulnerable, or the laws don't apply to them, it is a symptom that they are caught in an Infinite Loop of power. This loop shows up in the behavior of CEOs, as well as politicians, sports stars, and entertainers, just to name a few.

People lose the perspective of reality outside the loop in part because they are surrounded by people who do not challenge or contradict them. The Infinite Loop of power can lead to foolish mistakes, an arrogant demeanor, and the eventual downfall of that person and/or their organization. To a person who is not caught up in the loop, it is difficult to understand how someone could make such foolish choices, but to the person ensnared in the loop, it's like being surrounded by a bubble and protected from the realities of the world. There are frequent stories in the media about business people, sports stars, musicians, and politicians who are caught in Infinite Loop bubbles that seemingly protect them from reality. The examples include business executives that commit white-collar crimes, rock bands that destroy hotel rooms, sports stars that break the law, and politicians and their sexual indiscretions.

Take the example of Harry and Leona Helmsley, who built a billion-dollar real estate empire, including the Helmsley hotels. The Helmsleys, who thought they were protected by their perceived power, began to break the law by deliberately evading taxes. It is important to note that the taxes the Helmsleys did not pay were just a tiny fraction of their income. Why would these two wealthy business people risk jail for such a minuscule amount of money? It is possible that, in their Infinite Loop Thinking, money and power protected them from the laws that govern ordinary people.

The Infinite Loop of power also ensnares CEOs who listen only to the "yes men" who surround them. When CEOs are protected from negative feedback and minority viewpoints, they can lose touch with the real world. Smart executives (and other people in positions of power) know that when you are in the top position, it is essential to have someone who will question you, speak candidly, and even challenge you when needed. At IBM, Larry Ricciardi, senior vice president and corporate counsel, serves as that person for CEO Lou Gerstner. In an article for *Business Week*, Gerstner acknowledged Ricciardi's role and the importance of having candid feedback. "'Larry will always tell me what he thinks,' says Gerstner. 'I do not want people around me who tell me . . . what they think I want to hear.'" (Sager and Brady, 1999, p. 107)

Philip Condit, chairman and CEO of Boeing Co., is another top executive who recognizes the dangers of isolation. Condit regularly solicits feedback from Boeing's employees, asking them for opinions about the organization, and the marketplace. In Condit's view, the more sources of data he has access to, the less insulated he is, and the better his decisions.

ARROGANCE LOOPS

Organizations that hold a dominant or monopolistic position in an industry are prone to Infinite Loop Thinking. Although industry dominance allows the company to be very successful, it eventually leads to an Infinite Loop caused by arrogance, and then to strategic stumbles and financial problems. As the old saying goes, "If you want to curse a company, give it 20 years of success."

Take the example of IBM. For many years, IBM was the market leader in mainframe computers and the leading provider of computers and computer software for business. But their Infinite Loop was that mainframe computers would never be replaced. Along came Apple Computer and its dream of putting a computer on every desktop. Even when the Apple brand was building raving fans, IBM continued in its loop of thinking that desktops could never compete with mainframes. The loop was further reinforced by IBM's viewpoint that an upstart like Apple Computer could never dream of competing with a corporate giant like IBM.

It's not difficult to understand how IBM could have constructed and then become ensnared in the mainframe Infinite Loop: it was one giant company that talked to other giant companies. Because IBM people interacted with people who only knew mainframes, few could envision a future where a stand-alone computer could have the computing power that would allow it to replace the functions of a mainframe. For IBM, the information they took in reinforced their loop that the mainframe computer would always be the bedrock of business computing, making it difficult for them to recognize the loop.

When companies begin to believe they are invincible—that no other company can compete with them—it is a sign that an Infinite Loop is operating. The Infinite Loop of arrogance causes companies to make unreasonable demands, and to take customers for granted. Sometimes the Infinite Loop of arrogance does not become evident until a company begins the downward slide. Such is the case of Motorola, which in 2001 posted the company's first quarterly net loss in over 16 years. According to an article titled, "Motorola Goes Into Mea Culpa Mode to Atone for Its Cellphone Blunders," in *The Wall Street Journal*:

> *Motorola made some well-publicized strategic mistakes. . . . But what really undid Motorola in the cellphone business is what Verizon Wireless chief marketing officer John Stratton calls Motorola's "arrogance." Motorola made the dangerous mistake of forgetting that its customers weren't just the people carrying their phone but the wireless carriers as well. It is the carriers who determine which phones they will offer in their retail stores and which ones they will promote with special offers. At the height of its cockiness in the mid-1990s, when its StarTAC model was hot, Motorola dictated how carriers had to display some of its phones in their own stores. [Peterson, 2001, p. 1]*

The Wall Street Journal article went on to say that wireless carriers characterized Motorola as a "bossy, know-it-all supplier, a holdover from the days when the company was the market leader with the hottest products." (Peterson, 2001, p. 1)

When a company is a market leader, a monopoly, or part of a regulated industry, it's easy for the company to become a victim of an Infinite Loop. The actions of companies like Microsoft, AT&T (before the breakup), utility companies, and cable companies show the symptoms of a loop. Remember the days before satellite dishes, when cable companies had no competition? Because cable companies knew that customers had no other choices, service was terrible. If you wanted to have cable installed, you had to wait several weeks for an appointment. And you had to block off an entire day, to wait for the installer to show up. Taking customers for granted is one symptom of an Infinite Loop caused by monopolistic practices.

Corporate arrogance also appears when a company's management team thinks it has all the answers. In this situation, the Infinite Loop becomes something like a mantra for a company. The mantra may include statements about the strengths or weaknesses of competitors, about characteristics of the marketplace, or about the needs and wants of customers. Unfortunately, the mantras are too often invalid, and the loop prevents contradictory information from getting through.

Xerox is another in the long line of companies that became the victim of Infinite Loop Thinking. Did you know that Xerox scientists discovered the algorithms that are the basis for much of the computer programming people use today? Did you know that scientists at Xerox's Palo Alto Research Center (Xerox PARC) developed the graphical interface used by Macs and Windows, and invented the laser printer?

Did you know, also, that Xerox failed to capitalize on the discoveries made by their own scientists? Stuck in an Infinite Loop about the marketplace, the leadership of Xerox failed to see the early signs of what today is a booming market for home and small business computing, including laser and inkjet printers, and fax machines. In fact, Xerox is notorious for dismissing the inventions developed by PARC scientists—inventions that were then successfully marketed by other companies.

Luckily there are techniques for snipping an Infinite Loop of arrogance. One method is to spend time listening to customers. However, for this technique to work, top management has to be part of the team listening to customers. It doesn't work if it is just market researchers or salespeople who are doing the listening. Motorola has chosen this technique as part of its strategy to break out of the arrogance loop.

Another way to snip an Infinite Loop is to change perspective by asking thoughtful questions, like Andy Grove, former CEO of Intel, did in 1985 when Intel was struggling with the downward spiral of the market for computer memory. This technique only works if the people at the top are willing to seriously consider the questions. In Intel's case, it worked brilliantly. Grove talks about Intel's downward spiral in his book, *Only the Paranoid Survive*: "We had been losing money on memories for quite some time while trying to compete with the Japanese producers' high-quality, low-priced, mass-produced parts. But because business had been so good, we just kept at it, looking for the magical answer that would give us a premium price. We persevered because we could afford to. However, once business slowed down across the board and our other products couldn't take up the slack, the losses really started to hurt." (Grove, 1996, pp. 88–89)

Grove saw that Intel was stuck in a circular thinking loop. He saw that solving Intel's dilemma required a different perspective, so he asked a question that pushed the situation outside of the company's normal internal boundaries. This is Grove's recollection, from *Only the Paranoid Survive*:

*I remember a time in the middle of 1985 . . . I was in my office
with Intel's chairman and CEO, Gordon Moore, and we were discussing our quandary. Our mood was downbeat. I looked out the
window at the Ferris wheel of the Great America amusement park
revolving in the distance, then I turned back to Gordon and I
asked, "If we got kicked out and the board brought in a new CEO,
what do you think he would do?" Gordon answered without hesita-
tion, "He would get us out of memories." I stared at him, numb,
then said, "Why shouldn't you and I walk out the door, come back
and do it ourselves?" [Grove, 1996, p. 89]*

For Intel, shifting perspective resulted in snipping the loop.
By mid-1986, Intel was out of the memory business and into the mi-
croprocessor business. One year later, Intel was profitable once
again. And by 1996, it was the largest semiconductor company in
the world.

Sometimes snipping an organizational Infinite Loop requires
someone who is willing to take a risk to demonstrate the value of an
idea; someone who will nurture that idea until it reaches the point that
others can see its validity. Such is the case with one company that managed to snip its Infinite Loop, InSoft Incorporated. InSoft was created
in 1992 with the vision of developing a real-time video network that
would require only regular computers and an inexpensive desktop
camera. The company would accomplish this vision by using software
to replace the expensive hardware of other teleconferencing systems.
The partners of InSoft raised money from friends and acquaintances to
get the company up and running and eventually began generating several million dollars in corporate sales. At the time, the founders of In-
Soft, Dan Harple and Rich Pizzarro, were not intending to create a
product for use over the Internet.

Then the Internet blossomed. But, the InSoft board of directors
did not want to risk the cannibalization of their high-dollar corporate
sales ($7 million at that point) by developing a low-cost version that
could run over the Internet. Fortunately, Harple ignored the wishes of
the board of directors. He quietly started a below-the-radar project to
compress video for the Internet's limited bandwidth. Eventually,
Harple's Internet product led to the sale of InSoft to the Netscape company for $161 million.

PROCESS LOOPS

Infinite Loop Thinking is also prevalent in companies that are heavily looped into process. In some companies, there is a strong culture of creating and following processes. This is largely a desire for control in an environment that is uncertain. The lack of control pushes people to use any means they can to feel in control. Even if the control is just an illusion created by the process.

When companies are caught up in an Infinite Loop of process, the more that process is created, the more process people feel the need to create. This is because people expect the process to create control, so when control is not the result, they assume what is needed is more process. It's a perfect example of the saying, "You can never get enough of what you do not really want," meaning that if you are substituting process for control, you can never get enough process, since it doesn't produce what you really want (control).

It is not just large companies that fall prey to Infinite Loop Thinking. Even small companies get caught up in creating processes to try to control their environment. Processes are known, safe factors in a world of uncertainty and unknowns. So, it is natural for people to be more comfortable within the boundaries of a process than to venture into the unknown arena of taking action (and risks).

With so much time and energy invested in the process loop, very little real work gets accomplished. Instead of recognizing that action is needed instead of a process, the automatic response is, "We need a process for that." Every new process created carries with it the risk that people will forget the original reason for the process and get ensnared in the idea that the process itself is what's important.

Sometimes, an Infinite Loop of process is caused by the obsessive pursuit of a goal. Take the example of Burger King, embroiled in a desperate quest to create a new french fry that would put them on top in the world of fast food. In a 2001 article titled "Burger King's Decision to Develop French Fry Has Been a Whopper," *The Wall Street Journal* revealed: "To guarantee adequate crunch, Burger King included in its 19-page french fry specifications an unusual requirement that startled even veteran food scientists. For each mouthful of french fry, the degree of crispiness was to be 'determined by an audible crunch that should be present for seven or more chews . . . loud enough to be apparent to the evaluator.'" (Ordonez, 2001, p. 1) Unfortunately, as the preceding reference to specifications shows, the company got entangled in the process of engineering the ultimate french fry. And the obsession with the process didn't help the company. In spite of the hype and the years of development, sales began to fall less than one year after the introduction of the new french fry.

TALKING IN CIRCLES

The unknowns and uncertainties of today's business world can also paralyze companies by pushing them into Infinite Loops of analysis. When a company is in the throes of an Infinite Loop of analysis, people concentrate on talk and analysis instead of decisions and action.

In some organizations, the analysis loop leads to discussing an idea instead of implementing it. When the rules of engagement in a group include unlimited discussion about an idea, decisions and action can take forever.

The loop of talk instead of action is typical in organizations where risk taking is discouraged. Because it is much less risky to discuss an idea than to make a decision and to implement one, a lot of time and energy is invested in discussion. Also, in a company that is risk averse, implementation is often held hostage to certainty. However, in today's ambiguous business world, certainty is a rare phenomenon, so companies try to find certainty by spending more time in discussion. Discussion, of course, leads to more questions, which leads to the need for more discussion to resolve the questions, and so the loop continues.

Uncertainty and risk avoidance also push organizations to demand definitive, quantitative proof before moving ahead with a new idea. This demand can lead to classic *analysis paralysis*, the inability to move forward because you're embroiled in the analysis of a problem or situation. Analysis paralysis prevents people from making decisions and from solving problems because the process never gets past the analysis stage into solution or implementation.

George Conrades, CEO of Akamai, is very aware of the danger of letting uncertainty cause paralysis. In an interview with *Harvard Business Review*, Conrades said, "The danger is that uncertainty can lead

ACTION TOOL: The Circular Box

The Circular Box action tool identifies the danger signals of an organizational Infinite Loop, and suggests strategies to snip the loop.

Your organization may be stuck in an Infinite Loop if:

▮ You only listen to a small group of people.

▮ You have elegant and meticulously documented processes.

▮ Your organization has a mantra.

▮ You dictate to your customers.

▮ You limit discussion to only a few alternatives.

▮ Outside experts and expert opinions are not welcome.

▮ You're so confident in your chosen direction that contingency plans are not even considered.

▮ There are beliefs within the organization that cannot be questioned.

▮ Employees are discouraged from rocking the boat.

▮ Outsiders are stereotyped as evil, weak, or stupid.

Strategies to break out of the circular box:

1. Appoint a corporate fool: Give someone the job of asking "stupid" questions about policies, processes, and assumptions.

2. Obsolete your company: Pretend your premiere product or service was just rendered obsolete by technology or an unexpected competitor. What would your company do instead?

3. Embark on a Customer Listening Tour: Pick several current and former customers and take them to lunch or make an appointment to talk on the phone. Ask them: What is changing in your business or industry? What is your biggest challenge right now? If you had a corporate genie, what would your three wishes be?

to paralysis. You can spend so much time trying to nail down all the possibilities and risks, you never get around to taking action. And if that happens—if you become indecisive—you're dead." (Carr, 2000, pp. 121–122)

There is another danger in the Infinite Loop of analysis—that of confusing motion with action. When you spend a lot of time researching and gathering data, having discussions, scheduling meetings, creating committees, and all of the other tasks that go along with analyzing a problem or idea, it's difficult not to feel like you are taking action. However, all those tasks are just motion—the precursor to action. Action is making the decision, solving the problem, or implementing.

Organizations can snip Infinite Loops of analysis by linking discussion to implementation. One way to make that link is to end each discussion with an agreement about next steps, identifying who will be accountable for action, and by setting deadlines. Another way to make that link is to allocate a certain percentage of time in every meeting to discuss how to apply ideas and implement decisions.

KEY POINTS

I When people are stuck in a thinking loop, obsessed with a problem or situation, they are unable to see alternative strategies.

I Worry loops and awfulizing are built on faulty assumptions woven in among valid conclusions.

I The overconfidence bias means that 15 percent of the time that people believe they are right, they are actually wrong.

I Perfectionistic thinking can trigger an Infinite Loop because it focuses on the extremes of needing to do something perfectly.

I If you are stuck in a perfectionist Infinite Loop, take small steps to snip the loop.

I In an Infinite Loop, people think about an idea the same way, over and over.

KEY POINTS *(Continued)*

I Groupthink is one example of an Infinite Loop shared by a group of people. Groupthink limits the ability of groups to think in different ways and can blind them to shifts and changes in the marketplace.

I People find it difficult to disagree openly with the majority viewpoint.

I Infinite Loops of arrogance cause people and organizations to suffer from illusions of invulnerability. It is important for executives to have someone who will question, speak candidly, and challenge.

I Infinite Loops of process are the result of desire for control in an uncertain environment or obsessive pursuit of a goal.

I Infinite Loops of analysis slow implementation and discourage risk taking; snip them by linking discussion to implementation.

6

BRAIN OPERATING PRINCIPLE 4: Mental Maps

People rely on Mental Maps, made up of assumptions and unwritten rules, as mental shortcuts

Even if you have perfect vision, you are using the mental equivalent of prescription eyeglasses to navigate the world. The prescription in your mental eyeglasses is unique to you. No one else sees the world with the same viewpoint. These eyeglasses are your Mental Maps.

To cope with the complexity of life, your brain builds groups of mental shortcuts, or Mental Maps. Mental Maps are made up of assumptions and unwritten rules that people rarely question, once they are developed. People build maps for activities like living in their families, going to school, driving, and working in their jobs.

Mental Maps are similar to the psychological concepts of schemas and scripts. Remember that schemas are people's organized patterns of knowledge about the world. Scripts are a particular type of schema. The concept of scripts was developed by psychologists Roger Schank and Robert Abelson, and it refers to people's patterns of knowledge about the expected actions and appropriate behavior in everyday settings. For example, Schank and Abelson created a detailed restaurant script, which outlines people's knowledge of the sequence and events involved in a typical visit to a restaurant. In other words, scripts tell people who is supposed to do what, to whom, and why in a particular situation.

Mental Maps, like schemas and scripts, set up expectations about how the world should operate. They also determine the focus of attention. Because of those dynamics, maps influence how individuals view people and situations, and they determine what people do not see, as well.

Although each individual has their own unique set of maps, people share parts of maps—certain assumptions or unwritten rules—with others. Examining the rules of the road in a particular city or geographic area provides an easily understood illustration of shared unwritten rules. For example, when I moved to Wilmington, Delaware from Miami, Florida, I realized that in the east, when you are getting on a major highway, *merge* actually means "give up." Until I learned that unwritten rule, I nearly rear-ended several cars on the highway entrance ramps, because my unwritten rule was to watch the traffic, looking for a hole big enough for my car, and then follow the literal direction of that yellow sign that says, "merge."

We are fascinated with the reactions of strangers to our culture when they bump up against these Mental Maps. How many books or movies can you name that feature a character who is ignorant of society's rules for some reason? We laughed at E.T., as he explored the contents of the refrigerator, drank a few beers, and watched game shows on TV. We chuckled at Darryl Hannah's mermaid character in Splash, when she bit into her lobster, shell and all, in a fancy restaurant. We cheered Crocodile Dundee, as he won the heart of the sophisticated New Yorker, in spite of his rough edges and ignorance of big city etiquette.

MAPS AS AGREEMENTS

Your maps are agreements with yourself about how you should behave and how the world is supposed to behave. Maps determine what you see and perceive. They help you to interpret the world. They also determine your reactions to specific events. Every action you take makes sense if maps are taken into account.

It is important to recognize that many of the assumptions that make up your maps, you did not even consciously choose. You learned them as you grew up, from people like parents, teachers, coaches, and friends, and you continue to learn them today, from colleagues and bosses.

How did you learn the assumptions that make up your maps? You learned them from watching how your parents acted and interacted, from what they told you about how things should and shouldn't be. When your parents told you to sit up straight, don't talk with food in your mouth, wait to speak until you are spoken to, do not touch someone else's property without permission, turn the lights off when you're done, each of the statements helped to shape your maps.

You also learned assumptions from trial and error. You found out the obvious things, like a hot stove and skin aren't compatible. You learned the rules of gravity by building block towers, standing on the edge of the couch, or trying to roller skate. Eventually you began to learn more sophisticated concepts through trial and error.

One of the fascinating parts of watching children is to see them build their maps by testing the boundaries, trying things out, and asking questions. The endless strings of Why? Why? Why? questions are a child's way of building those maps. By the time people become adults, they have built thousands of assumptions and unwritten rules into maps of how they should behave and how the world works.

For example, somewhere along the way, you may have learned that cold calling is an unpleasant experience, to be avoided at all costs. Some people learned to be intimidated by authority figures, while others learned to flaunt authority. A few lucky people learned to treat rejection as a challenge, while the rest of us view it with reactions that range from unpleasant to horrified.

Every person sees the world in their own unique way, because each person has their own unique atlas of maps. You do share some assumptions, rules, and parts of your maps with others. If you were raised in the same family, went to the same school, belong to the same religion, come from the same culture, work in the same company, or in the same profession, you share parts of maps with others. But even family members only share pieces of maps, not an entire atlas.

Oddly enough, sharing pieces of your maps can sometimes create problems in understanding. Because you share pieces with someone, you assume they see the world exactly as you do. When disagreements do happen, they are jarring. When an individual thinks they understand someone—how that person thinks, and their viewpoint of the world—and that person says or does something that does not fit, it's a shock and is difficult to understand.

The fact that each person has a unique atlas of maps explains why everyone inhabits their own reality. No one else can experience the world in exactly the same way as another. This is why it is sometimes difficult to understand other people's viewpoints—even when it is someone that you know well. However, if you can understand that person's maps, it helps to make sense of what they say and do. Every action makes sense when it is overlaid with the assumptions or unwritten rules from a map.

IDENTIFYING MAPS

One of the most effective techniques to enhancing your thinking skills—whether your goal is innovation, making a change, decreasing stress, or working better with another person—is to identify your own assumptions and rules.

It is almost impossible to identify the rules of every map in your atlas, because each person has thousands of rules that impact how they think and act in the situations in their life. The key is to identify the maps that are impacting a particular area of your life (such as how you do your job or the rules of your industry) and then to articulate the rules that make up each of those maps. Once you start paying attention to your maps and those of others, you will be surprised at how often clues show up. When a person says something like, "I think we should do it this way," or "Aren't you going to do X before you do Y?" or "You're supposed to," or "I can't do that," it reveals pieces of their maps.

Take a look at your own assumptions. What do you think of someone who tells you they went to an Ivy League school? What about when someone tells you they are an artist? What if they tell you they work for the government? What do you think if someone grew up in a small, rural town? What about if they grew up in a big city? What if someone married at 18? Or someone is not married at 40? In each of these scenarios, you make assumptions about that person based on a single piece of information. A handy shortcut for your brain, but one that doesn't always serve your best interest.

Looking at your assumptions helps you to identify your own maps. It's important to identify maps because they affect so much of what people do in their lives. They affect your ability to change, your ability to make decisions, and your ability to work with people who think and act differently than you.

Here are just a few examples of the maps many people rely upon to function in everyday life. Each of these maps contain a list of rules—a list that may be short or long, old or new, useful or outdated.

General

I Men are . . . not emotional; bad housekeepers; good with mechanical things.

I Women are . . . not logical; too emotional; good with people; maternal.

I The world is . . . friendly; hostile; connected; unfair.

I Life is . . . difficult; a journey; a test; a bowl of cherries.

I Money is . . . the root of all evil; happiness; power; to be saved for a rainy day.

Business

I Bosses are . . . always right; a pain in the neck; never satisfied; brown-nosers.

I Customers are . . . always right; a pain the neck; demanding; disloyal.

I Business should be . . . logical; conservative; fun; profitable.

As difficult as it is to identify your maps, it is important to work at identifying some of your assumptions and unwritten rules, so you can determine if they are hindering or helping you. For example, people of the Baby-Boom generation sometimes struggle with Mental Maps that hinder them when they become entrepreneurs. Because boomers grew up in a world dominated by large, corporate businesses, their ideas about how business should operate were influenced by the rules of big business. So, when a boomer becomes an entrepreneur, the assumptions they make about their customers, their employees, and their business policies are based on what worked in the days of big business, not necessarily what works in today's environment.

Maps acquired in one business setting are not always compatible with the maps in a new office or company. For example, Charles is a partner in a small, entrepreneurial business. In business, Charles relies on policies he learned from the corporate environment—policies such as set working hours, no celebrations during the working day, and rigid job descriptions. Unfortunately, these policies do not work as well in a small business as they do in big business. Because the policies are too restrictive and inflexible, Charles has difficulty motivating and retaining his employees. His maps, influenced by what he views as appropriate for business, conflict with the reality of his current situation. My suggestion to Charles was that he research policies in companies that were more similar to his, instead of looking to large corporations that were very different for examples. Once he did, Charles realized that his old assumptions were causing problems, and he and his partner revised the restrictive policies.

MAPS AND CHANGE

The principle of Mental Maps helps you understand why people struggle with change. When the environment changes in some way, people and events don't act in the way the maps that you've relied upon say they should. You have to learn to redraw your maps to understand the changes (the new environment) and that is a process easier said than done.

People do not just simply erase the old maps and replace them with new, as William Bridges points out in his book, *Transitions*: "Separated from the old identity and the old situation or some important aspect of it, a person floats free in a kind of limbo between two worlds. But there is still the reality in that person's head—a picture of the 'way things are,' which ties the person to the old world with subtle strands of assumption and expectation." (Bridges, 1980, p. 98) During the transition process, you have to deal with the confusion between the old maps and the new.

People need to struggle through the confusion of being in limbo between two worlds, however, because when the world changes and their maps do not, their maps can block them from succeeding in that new world, causing stress, and influencing them to make poor decisions. Maps, like schemas, determine what people see and don't see, and expectations for how the world should behave. Although people have always had to deal with changes in their lives that impacted their Mental Maps, technology has intensified the amount and the rate of change, particularly in the business world. In the last five years especially, the maps that businesses and business people relied on to become successful have been turned upside down and inside out.

Just think about the impact the Internet has on your work. It has changed (and is still changing) the way you deal with colleagues and customers. It gives you access to information that you never dreamed of. It has also changed the buying habits of your customers, whether you sell to consumers or to other businesses.

Do you feel like the pace of your world has sped up? You are not alone. It used to be that there was time to think before you had to respond. But today, with faxes, pagers, cell phones, voice mail, e-mail, and the Web, people are used to information at the snap of their fingers. Which means that your customers, whether they are internal or external, expect you to provide instant information and instant answers.

These are just a couple of examples in a world of changes people are experiencing during this economic shift. One of the reasons that these changes are particularly difficult is that past experience in business (maps built through experience) led people to believe certain assumptions were true, but today's economy requires people to change those assumptions.

To make the shift even more difficult, for many of the new assumptions there is little solid proof that the changes are absolutely required for success, because the environment is still evolving. When your experience tells you one thing and the environment is giving you signals to go a different way, the maps you have built through experience add a degree of difficulty to the change.

Maps make change more difficult because, over the years, you have layered rules on beliefs on assumptions. Your experiences in the world validated those maps. When your experiences didn't agree with your maps, you may have dismissed it as a fluke experience or something you misunderstood. In some cases, if an experience did not jibe with your maps, you outright ignored it. In fact, there are numerous psychological studies that show people literally do not see something that doesn't fit their maps. For example, in one study, Jerome Bruner and Leo Postman of Harvard used the tachistoscope (a machine that flashes images quickly, sometimes as briefly as a hundredth of a second) to show people very brief views of playing cards, most of which were standard but some of which were not, like a red four of spades.

Habit and expectation caused twenty-seven of their twenty-eight subjects to see the abnormal cards as normal." (Hunt, 1994, p. 449)

Change is also difficult because you have to go through a process of changing your assumptions to change your maps. To do that successfully requires that you do not ignore information that is incongruent with your maps, which means that during the change process you have to hold two conflicting beliefs in your mind, and handle the dissonance.

Because of maps and the discomfort that changing beliefs causes, people are more comfortable with the familiar—even if the familiar is painful—rather than the new, even though the something new might promise great benefits. It may be difficult to understand this concept logically, but it is a very important point, particularly for managers and sales professionals. Employees may be unhappy in their jobs, but stay because they assume a known quantity is better than an unknown one. Customers may stay with current suppliers, even those that do not completely meet their needs, because they have working relationships with the suppliers and those relationships are more comfortable than starting anew.

MAPS AND DECISIONS

Mental Maps impact assumptions and risk taking when decisions are being made. Maps affect what you pay attention to in a decision situation, the factors you ignore or discount, and your assumptions of cause and effect. Since maps are the lens through which you view the world, they affect how you evaluate a decision or risk. The way that one person views a decision or risk can be completely different than another, because of the different lenses of their maps.

Because of the impact of maps on decision making, it is important to articulate the assumptions used to evaluate a decision. When you articulate assumptions, it helps you to see the factors that are influencing your decision, even if the influences are unconscious. In fact, you might be surprised at how much decision making is based on unconscious influences and assumptions that we all take for granted.

Have you ever been part of a group evaluation of a decision and just could not understand why another member of the group did not see the decision your way? Maps explain why committee decisions are difficult, because different maps cause people to evaluate decisions in different ways. Each person sees the decision in relation to his or her own viewpoint of the world.

In this situation, it helps to articulate assumptions. Information and ideas that you take for granted may be unknown or not understood by someone else. When you articulate the assumptions you use in evaluating a decision, it helps other people understand your viewpoint. You can then find more points of agreement than disagreement, which smoothes the path for discussing the remaining areas of disagreement.

When you are selling to a customer, it is important to try to understand your customer's maps and how the factors they will use to make their decision relate to your product or service. Too often, people assume that what they believe is important is also important to their customers and that customers will use the same factors to make a purchasing decision.

For instance, one client of mine, David, is the developer of a new marketing technology. During discussions about the features and benefits that could be used to sell the product, David became impatient. "Why are we wasting so much time on this? If they can't see what an innovative technology this is, we shouldn't even be talking to them." David is blinded by a map that says innovative technology is everything—the old idea that if you build a better mousetrap, the world will beat a path to your door. He doesn't understand that to sell the new product, the business needs to show customers the link between the innovative technology and how it can benefit their business. Few customers will purchase innovative technology if they cannot understand how it fits with their business goals.

Maps also affect risk taking. Each person has maps that tell them when and whether to take a risk. When confronted with a risk, people ask themselves: "Is this a familiar or unfamiliar risk?" "If I've taken a similar risk before, how did it work out?" "What happened the last time I took a risk?" "Have I seen someone else take a similar risk?" Maps determine if a risk is worth the benefit for an individual. What is worthwhile for one person (based on their map) isn't necessarily worthwhile for another.

MAPS AND WORKING RELATIONSHIPS

Understanding your own maps and learning to detect the maps of others is particularly important when you are working with colleagues and customers. Working from different maps causes misunderstand-ings, conflict, and miscommunication. When two people have a diffi-cult time working together, it's a pretty good bet that they are working from radically different maps.

A good example of misunderstandings that are a function of dif-ferent maps comes from my own work experience. When I went to work for a global ad agency, one of my colleagues and I did not see eye to eye. Within a few months of my joining the firm, we actively dis-liked one another. Whenever I would bring up ideas or client projects in a meeting, Carol would go on the attack. She would fire off ques-tions that seemed to be designed to portray my ideas as shortsighted, inadequate, or outright stupid. When Carol went into attack mode, I would become defensive and either fire back or just withdraw. As you can imagine, staff meetings were not productive experiences when the two of us were armed and dangerous.

Finally, one day, I approached her and said, "We need to figure this out." I explained to her that her questioning felt like an attack. She countered that she was just trying to understand my ideas and pro-jects. As we continued to talk, I learned that Carol grew up in a family of lawyers, where debate at the dinner table was the usual mode of op-eration. She had learned, growing up, the art of cross-examination, and had perfected her skill in a working environment that valued asking pointed questions. She also admitted that she did feel a little intimi-dated by my new role in the agency, so she might have been question-ing me with more fervor than she did others. After learning about each other's maps, the two of us called a truce. Carol agreed to rein in her cross-examination and I agreed to take her questions in the spirit of curiosity instead of criticism. Carol and I became working teammates instead of adversaries.

When you are working with other people, you spend a lot of time making assumptions and guesses about them. Remember that attribu-tion theory says people make inferences about other people, and those inferences impact feelings and behavior. Mostly, you are not even aware that you are making assumptions, because you've been doing it for so much of your life. You make an assumption that you know what someone wants from you. You guess at the hidden meanings behind their words or actions. You guess at their motives. You make guesses about what someone thinks of you. But you forget that the guesses you make about other people are never 100 percent accurate, because of the differences in maps.

The concept of integrity illustrates how maps can be radically different. Integrity illustrates maps on two levels: first, in the perception of the meaning of the word; and second, in the assumptions people make about other people. Integrity is a concept that people have come to define as adherence to high standards, morals, or values, usually standards that conform to one's own maps. When someone else violates the rules of the integrity map, people label them as lacking in integrity. However, the word *integrity* actually has the same root word as integration, and means adherence to a code or standard of values, or the condition of being whole or undivided. It does not necessarily mean adherence to society's map of integrity.

I like to use this concept as an illustration of how different our maps can be. I tell people that if someone grows up believing that stealing is okay—because they learned from their parents that stealing was the only way to survive or to assert control over their world—then that person has integrity when they steal. This idea provokes a strong reaction from most people. People who have rigid maps have a difficult time with the idea that someone who steals can have integrity.

Our maps can be radically different, particularly in this new business environment, where we are working in groups of diverse people. The diversity may be age, culture, race, gender, background, education, or a combination of factors. The diversity is more evident in businesses now because of the amount of teamwork, the number of group projects, and the reduction in top-down direction that are characteristic of this new environment. When people work closely together in teams or groups, it creates more opportunity for differences in maps to cause conflict and misunderstanding.

The conflicts between the boomer generation and younger generations in the workplace have received a lot of attention. I hear these generational complaints about Generation Xers from boomer managers in the workplace. The conflicts are the result of different maps. Boomers grew up steeped in the old economy rules that said: Work hard, pay your dues, do a good job and you'll have a job; don't ask questions, don't challenge your seniors, and don't get too big for your britches. The younger generation, on the other hand, who grew up watching their parents lose their jobs for no concrete reason after sacrificing for years, learned to question everything, expect people to prove themselves worthy before being given respect, and expect instant gratification or something for nothing.

One of most-voiced complaints by boomers about Generation Xers is that they have no work ethic. Actually Generation Xers have a strong work ethic, but they are motivated by different things than their parents. Xers are more entrepreneurial in their viewpoint toward work. They are willing to invest their energy, time, and talent in an enterprise if they see the appropriate reward. But they won't knock themselves out for some vague promise of reward and security like boomers did. Xers are more likely to prefer working independently, either as an independent contractor or as an intrapreneur in an organization. They are more interested in performance and results than in politics and paying dues. Generation Xers are also more likely to view security as having options, not commitments, and mobility instead of stability.

Although the first reaction when you come across a person with different maps is to tally the reasons why that different map is wrong, a more effective strategy is to try to understand the maps and rules that person is using to navigate the world. If you can understand someone else's maps, you can work at finding common ground.

MAPPING EXPECTATIONS

You can use the principle of Mental Maps to help other people understand you better by investing the time and energy to make your expectations, your intentions, or your purpose clear in your interactions. Articulating expectations, intentions, and purpose improves relationships, whether it is with your colleagues, the people you supervise, or your customers.

What does articulating expectations mean? When you are working with a colleague, articulating expectations means talking about how you expect to work together, what you need from one another, and what you expect from your working relationship. When you are supervising someone, articulating expectations means explaining how you expect work to be done, and what are your priorities. When you are working with customers, articulating expectations involves explaining the process of the work—what comes after what—explaining what your customers can expect of you, and what you need from your customers.

When people do not articulate expectations and, instead, assume that other people see the world exactly as they do, they are setting themselves up for conflict, for problems, and for misunderstandings. Why do people resist articulating their expectations? One reason is that it takes time and energy away from what people view as their real work. Another reason is that articulating expectations is difficult because it requires a person to sit down and really think about the outcome and the process of the work.

One client, Spencer, is the CEO of a mail-order company. He started the company from scratch and it has grown to be an organization of about 100 people. One day we met for a coaching session and he spent the entire session lamenting the fact that no one in his organization ever did what he wanted them to do, and if they did, they didn't do it in the way he wanted it done. I asked him, "Have you articulated your expectations?" He paused for a minute and said, "I don't know what you mean." So, I elaborated, "Have you sat down with your staff and told them what the priorities are, and explained the process of how you want them to handle customers and projects?" He admitted that he hadn't. He thought for a minute, and then said, "But, I shouldn't have to. I'm the boss, they should figure it out."

This story always gets a knowing chuckle from audiences. They are accustomed to dealing with bosses who do not articulate expectations. It is also an excellent example of thinking that needs to change. In the past, people spent a lot of time trying to scope out the boss. "What does he want from me?" "What is she thinking?" "What mood is he in today?" However, in today's competitive environment, we do not have the time and talent to waste while people play the game, "What's the boss thinking today?" We need to learn to articulate expectations.

In addition to learning to articulate expectations, people also need to learn how to articulate their intentions or purpose. There is a dynamic in human interaction that goes like this: "I judge myself by my intentions and others by their actions." Think back to your last interaction with someone that turned into an argument or conflict. Did you feel misunderstood? Did you feel that the other person was attributing motives to you that were inaccurate, or that the conversation didn't turn out as you had intended?

Making your intentions and your purpose clear helps to illuminate your map for other people. When I work with teams that are having difficulty communicating or resolving conflict, I ask them to do an exercise during their meetings: Start every sentence with "My intention is . . ." as in "My intention in asking this question is . . ." or "My intention in contributing this information is. . . ." It is a time-consuming and sometimes frustrating process, but it does sharply raise people's awareness of how much people take for granted and misunderstand in their everyday interactions.

It is not necessary to make your intentions or purpose clear in every single interaction that takes place. But when you are trying to communicate in difficult circumstances, persuade someone, or clarify a conversation that's not going so well, stating intentions can make a world of difference.

ORGANIZATIONAL MAPS

Everyone likes to have road maps to follow. Maps tell people when to turn right or left, how many miles to the next exit, and which road will get them to their goal the fastest. But what happens when the map is outdated and there are new roads, or when the old roads no longer lead where you think they lead?

Like individuals, organizations use Mental Maps. Organizational maps are also made up of rules and assumptions. Assumptions about the industry the company belongs to, about the customers it sells to, and about the internal functioning of the organization itself. All these assumptions make up the organization's business concept.

The organization's assumptions and unwritten rules impact the strategy, products, and success of a business. Maps serve as a lens through which organizations see people, products, customers, and the marketplace. The expectations of an organization determine its business outcomes. In *Destination Z*, author Robert Baldock explains the impact of false Mental Maps in business: "Businesses which find their way around their markets based on maps made by forecasters (with an early eighteenth-century sense of their own infallibility) are in danger of having a totally false mental map of the area in which they operate. IBM at the beginning of the 1980s was just such a company. Its mental map of the computer industry contained all sorts of islands which Big Blue failed to see were all part of one contiguous continent." (Baldock, 1998, pp. 78–79)

The assumptions that business people make can help or hurt the business. All too often, they hurt because they blind business people to trends, shifts, and changes. History teaches great lessons about people who were blinded by their experience and assumptions.

A book called *The Experts Speak* is filled with examples of pronouncements from people who were blinded by their maps. Here are just a few:

- "We don't like their sound. Groups of guitars are on the way out." Decca Recording Company executive, turning down the Beatles, 1962.

- "Sensible and responsible women do not want to vote. The relative positions to be assumed by man and woman in the working out of our civilization were assigned long ago by a higher intelligence than ours." Grover Cleveland, former president of the United States, 1905.

- "Everything that can be invented has been invented." Charles H. Duell, commissioner of the U.S. Office of Patents, 1899.

- "When the Paris Exhibition closes, electric light will close with it and no more will be heard of it." Erasmus Wilson, professor at Oxford University, 1878.

- "Video won't be able to hold onto any market it captures after the first six months. People will soon get tired of staring at a plywood box every night." Darryl Zanuck, head of 20th Century-Fox Studios, c. 1946.

- "I think there is a world market for about five computers." Attributed to Thomas J. Watson, chairman of the board, IBM, 1943.

- "There is no reason for any individual to have a computer in their home." Ken Olson, president of Digital Equipment Corporation, speaking to the World Future Society, 1977.

(Cerf and Navasky, 1984, pp. 182, 75, 203, 203, 208, 208, 209)

SHARED MAPS

People that work in a common industry, company, or profession often share pieces of (if not entire) maps. These maps contain assumptions about their customers, about their products, and about how to get things done.

You know the people in the company who really know how to get things done? The ones who can circumvent the red tape and the politics and move a project along? Those are the people who understand the unwritten rules and maps the organization is operating from, even if they do not consciously recognize that understanding. They may not always follow the rules, but they know when it is most effective to follow them and when they need to break them.

A company's reaction to pressure or crisis provides clues to the company's maps. When a company's shared map is radically different from its customers' shared map, it is a pretty good bet that eventually the company will run into problems. Conflicts between corporate and customer maps are typical in strong scientific or technology cultures. The strength of maps dominated by a focus on research, discovery, and product features (instead of benefits), pushes customer maps into a murky background.

One of the reasons that Intel struggled with the chip controversy related earlier in this book is that Intel has a strong scientific map that is taken for granted across the company. That map says something like, "Judge everything against the science; if the science says it's not a problem, then it's not a problem." Unfortunately, the customers who bought computers with Intel inside did not share that scientific map. Instead, their maps said, "Big companies will take advantage of insignificant consumers at every opportunity." When you consider the conflicts between those two maps, it is easy to see why a small problem turned into a big issue.

Companies have trouble seeing outside the boundaries of their maps. Often, the people in the best position to see outside are those who are listened to least by a company. These people include the receptionists and employees in call centers that take inbound customer calls and the sales professionals who talk to customers every day and who see customers in their native habitat.

Upper level managers sometimes discount the views of these people because of perceived status in the company. If a salesperson's viewpoint on customers does not match the market research, the quantitative data of the research often wins out. A manager will rationalize this decision with the reasoning that a salesperson is not in a position to see the business' big picture or that they are too close to the customer to view the situation objectively. But, sometimes managers who make written policy are disconnected from the everyday realities of their customers.

CULTURE MAPS

The culture of an organization is influenced by the maps of the company's leadership because the leadership creates a vision, structure, values, and processes, based on its viewpoint of the business environment and how the business fits in that environment. These elements provide the basis for organizational culture. The leadership (consciously or unconsciously) teaches assumptions and unwritten rules to employees through its business viewpoint.

Maps also provide a decoder for understanding a particular organization. Identifying the unwritten rules and assumptions of an organization produces a picture of how that company operates, how it views customers, and how it sees its marketplace. The stronger the culture, the more visible the maps.

Maps are taught in organizations in many ways. Remember, just because the rules are unwritten doesn't mean they are unspoken. Listening to the conversations of employees can provide a lot of clues to an organization's maps. When a group of people criticize a colleague, chances are the person being criticized has broken a rule or two in the organization's map. When an employee tells another employee, "Better not do that" or "You'll be more successful if . . ." the rules are being passed from one person to another.

It is not just the words of the conversation that provide clues, it is also how the discussion itself is structured. Is criticism hushed and hidden or discussed openly? Are hallway and doorway discussions the norm or do conversations only take place behind closed doors? Is it the senior employees who have a stranglehold on the prevailing opinions or are new, younger employees given credibility as well? The nonverbal cues are as loaded with information as the words themselves.

Organizations also communicate their maps through storytelling. The stories that are told in a company, whether they feature heroes or villains, teach assumptions and unwritten rules. Southwest Airlines has a Culture Committee, made up of more than 100 storytellers who are the company's cultural ambassadors and missionaries. The committee includes representatives of many different areas of the business, from flight attendants and reservationists to top executives. In *Nuts! Southwest Airlines' Crazy Recipe for Business and Personal Success*, authors Kevin and Jackie Freiberg describe the makeup of the committee. "It is not a group of headquarters staff and managers who use the power to tell the rest of the organization how they ought to think and behave. Rather it is a group of shamans, spiritual teachers and organizational storytellers." (Freiberg and Freiberg, 1998, p. 165)

Identifying the unwritten rules and assumptions in an organization requires investigation, active listening, and reading between the lines. Why would you want to go to the trouble of identifying a company's unwritten rules and assumptions? First, because they help you successfully navigate the organization—whether you are an employee trying to implement a program or an outside supplier trying to sell a solution to a company's problem. Second, because unwritten rules and assumptions provide an early warning system for threats to the company's future.

The strength and the danger of unwritten rules are clearly illustrated in General Motor's unwritten rules, as identified by James O'Toole, author and vice president of the Aspen Institute. O'Toole studied the operating assumptions of GM and wrote about them in his book, *Leading Change*. O'Toole noted that many of these assumptions were developed in the early 1900s, but were still in use during the 1980s.

Look at a few of the unwritten rules O'Toole identified and see if you can pinpoint where these rules might have served as early warning signals of danger.

I **Cars are primarily status symbols. Styling is therefore more important than quality to buyers who are, after all, going to trade up every other year.**

I **The American car market is isolated from the rest of the world. Foreign competitors will never gain more than 15 percent of the domestic market.**

I Workers do not have an important impact on productivity or product quality.

I Consumer, environmental, and other social concerns are unimportant to the American public. (O'Toole, 1995, p. 179)

Of course, the picture in the strategic rearview mirror is always clearer than the one down the road. But an organization that identifies its own unwritten rules and then makes a habit of questioning and challenging them is less likely to be blindsided by shifts in the environment or the marketplace. It is also more likely to mitigate the negative impacts of unwritten rules on working relationships, innovation, and productivity.

One of the exercises I like to do with groups is to ask them to identify the unwritten rules of their own organizations. Here is just a sample of the organizational unwritten rules we've surfaced.

I The savior gets rewarded, the herald gets the cold shoulder.

I Don't brag on yourself.

I Dot your i's and cross your t's.

I Tell the boss whatever he or she wants to hear.

I Don't have conflict. If you do have conflict, you are not a team player.

I Check your problems at the door when you arrive at work, do whatever it takes to please the customer, then pick up your problems at the door when you leave.

I Don't be the bearer of bad news.

I Don't talk to *my* customers/clients.

Some managers might feel these are fairly harmless (or even beneficial) rules. But the rules can have unintended negative effects. Take the common unwritten rule, left over from the old command and control days, that says "Don't have conflict." This is a rule that I see again and again in companies that have difficulty working in teams or encouraging innovation. Instead of judging people on their ability to manage and productively resolve conflict, companies create an unrealistic expectation that people can function without any conflict whatsoever. So the people who have conflict (whether resolved or not) are frowned upon.

The problem is that not allowing conflict leads to stale ideas, bad decisions, and a lack of innovation. It is a common symptom of the lemming effect: an entire team or business jumps over the cliff because no one can raise conflicting opinions about a program or direction for fear of being viewed as not a team player and penalized.

People who don't have conflict turn to passive-aggressive behavior: they take their grievances underground or stuff them in their emotional sacks. But, at some point the grievances have to come out, and when they do, the grievances are more troublesome than if they had been dealt with in the first place.

ACTION TOOL: Take Me to Your Leader

Use the Take Me to Your Leader action tool to identify your individual and organizational assumptions and unwritten rules.

You have been chosen as the Earthling host to an alien, who has just arrived from Mars, and must integrate itself into today's business world. The alien will be working in a job very similar to yours in your organization. What assumptions and rules would you need to teach your guest? What would you tell your alien guest about what to do or not to do to be successful? What would you tell it about your customers? Your company? Your industry?

Here is a list of questions to help jumpstart your thinking:

▌ What behaviors are encouraged or discouraged?

▌ What are the rules about time (Be on time for meetings; Don't waste time; Don't be seen just thinking; What time to arrive for work and what time to leave)?

▌ What are the rules about asking questions? (Are there particular subjects that are off limits? Are there certain people you don't question?)

ACTION TOOL: Take Me to Your Leader *(Continued)*

▌ What happens when someone makes a mistake?

▌ What do people talk about when they talk informally about work?

▌ What policies can be broken without punishment?

▌ What policies absolutely cannot be violated?

▌ Do people put most of their time and energy into politics or results?

▌ What are the rules about disagreement and conflict?

▌ What happens when someone brings up a new idea?

▌ What behaviors and accomplishments are talked about in performance reviews?

▌ Is there a dress code? What is it? What happens when it is broken?

▌ Why do your customers buy your products/services?

▌ What are your competitors' strengths and weaknesses?

▌ What one thing could your competitors do that would put you out of business?

▌ What would happen if your biggest product or service became obsolete?

▌ Why aren't your non-customers your customers?

▌ When and why do your customers fire your company?

▌ Why do you work for your company and not a competitor?

Here is one more hint: As you are thinking about what advice you would give to your new friend, you'll know you are on the right track if you use the words:

▌ Should.

▌ Shouldn't.

▌ Can't.

▌ Don't.

▌ Do it this way.

BLENDING MAPS

When two organizations join together, whether it is through acquisition or merger, the leadership invests a lot of energy and time in planning how to mesh the products, buildings, equipment, processes, job titles, and so on. What leaders often fail to plan for is how to mesh the two cultures—the maps that make up the business concepts of the two organizations. There is a prevailing expectation that if the meshing of the building blocks of the business (which few managers define as including the people) are figured out, the rest will fall into place.

Unfortunately, blending cultures is not as easy as putting the right-shaped block in the same-shaped hole. First, too many organizations are not aware of the unwritten rules and assumptions that make up their maps and their culture. Second, of the organizations that are aware, few invest much time or effort in teaching people how to navigate a new culture. Third, few organizations recognize the impact of conflicting cultures on the productivity of the new organization.

Conflicts in culture can be major or minor. They include unwritten rules and assumptions about such things as risk taking, going over someone else's head, when it is okay to disagree with a colleague, who should be kept informed about what, taking initiative, how deadlines are viewed, what takes place in meetings, and whether the primary focus is on internal processes or external customers. These kinds of conflicts between maps can derail an acquisition or merger or, at the very least, hamper the ability of the new organization to live up to the financial expectations created by the merger or acquisition.

Discounting the impact of organizational maps may account for the fact that many mergers fail to achieve their expected financial results. Mercer Management Consulting reported in the January 1997 issue of the *Economist* that a study of 300 major mergers found that in 57 percent of the merged companies return to shareholders lagged behind the average for their industries.

Here are some examples of how these cultural differences created problems in blending organizations:

I The 1997 merger of Boeing and McDonnell Douglas was hampered by a culture clash between the top people.

I In acquiring small start-up companies, Motorola found that the culture clash between the acquired companies and Motorola kept the company from benefiting fully from the acquisitions. The smaller companies were accustomed to a more cooperative culture, were more outwardly focused on customers and marketing, and tended to be more homogenous.

I Apria Healthcare, formed by the 1995 merger of Homedco Group and Abbey Healthcare, struggled in blending two very different cultures—one entrepreneurial and one more conservative.

I The cultural differences between German business practices and American business practices contributed to the problems in the multibillion-dollar merger of Daimler Benz and Chrysler Corporation in 1998.

Cisco and GE Capital are two companies that recognize the importance of helping people learn the unwritten rules and adapt to a new culture. For example, when Cisco makes an acquisition, it sends out an integration team to help the acquired company's employees understand the processes of Cisco, how the company works, and how to get things done in the Cisco culture.

GE Capital also recognizes the importance of teaching culture when making acquisitions. Not only does GE Capital designate an integration manager to work with the people of the acquired company, it also holds a three-day "cultural workout session."

The integration manager gives people in the newly-acquired company someone they can freely ask questions of, someone who can decode the rules of how things work at GE Capital, and someone who can act as a guide to the new culture. The integration manager translates the culture and business customs of GE Capital for the people in the acquired company and also translates the culture and business customs of the acquired company for the people of GE Capital.

In addition to the services of the integration manager, GE Capital holds a session with key people from GE Capital and the management team of the acquired company to "talk about the history of their companies, the folklore, and the heroes that made them what they are. That leads to focused discussions about cultural differences

and similarities and their implications for doing business—for instance, how to go to market, how much to focus on cost, or how
concepts of authority differ." (Ashkenas, DeMonaco, and Francis,
1998, p. 177)

MAPS AND EXPECTATIONS

In organizations, articulating expectations is important, just as it
is in person-to-person relationships. Developing vision, mission,
and value statements is one way that organizations articulate their
expectations.

I believe that many organizations make two mistakes in developing vision, mission, and value statements. First, they make the
statements as brief as possible, perhaps because they believe that
a short statement is all that employees can remember. Second,
they dress up the language in search of words that convey the importance of the statement. Therefore, statements turn out to be
ambiguous, making it difficult for employees to use them to guide
their actions.

One of the clearest articulations of expectations that I have
seen is in the values statement developed by PSS/World Medical,
Inc. In his book, *Faster Company*, PSS founder and former CEO
Patrick Kelly outlines what PSS calls the Top 20. Here are a few
points from the Top 20:

I Service all our customers like they are the only ones we have.

I Recognize our people as the most valuable asset.

I Always communicate without fear of retribution.

I Encourage ideas and creativity at all levels.

I Provide an environment of trust and honesty.

I Minimize excuses and maximize getting the job done.

I Suggest and encourage better ways of doing things.

I Minimize paperwork and memos. (Kelly, P., 1998, p. 112)

In developing the Top 20, PSS obviously didn't worry about brevity. And notice how the language is clear, simple, and direct.

Articulating expectations is especially important when an organization is struggling through a major change. Unfortunately, this is the time when many leaders don't do the hard work of spelling out the expectations. Because of the leftover maps from many years of learning to treat people and organizations like machines, the tendency in organizational change is to set a goal or outcome for the change, and then just expect it to happen. Naming the outcome without helping people understand the expectations of how to get to that outcome is a little like throwing first-time swimmers in the deep end of a pool and expecting them to swim: a few will figure it out, but many more will drown.

Articulating expectations is not the same as telling people what to do, giving them orders, or micro-managing. Articulating expectations means building the bridge between where the organization is and where it needs to be. It is helping people understand how to make a lot of small changes that will add up to the big shift.

Articulating expectations also improves the working relationships of teams. For teams, articulating expectations includes articulating their ground rules or operational guidelines for working together. As humans, people make a natural assumption that other people, particularly those in the same profession or industry, have the same maps. When people don't act as expected because they are working from different maps, it causes problems.

The management team of a technology company was struggling to communicate, which hampered their effectiveness in working as a team. People arrived at meetings without having read the agenda or done necessary preparation, discussions turned into arguments, and projects slipped further and further behind. Difficult as it was for a company that was dominated by a technology-first-and-foremost map to recognize, the fact that 15 people were operating from 15 very different maps (with no common map for the team) was contributing to the production delays and the sliding revenues of this business.

My first step in working with the team was to help them understand the shift in the business world that made communications and working relationships much more critical than in the past. Then, gradually, we started developing a shared map and common language for the team. We worked through the articulation of expectations for team meetings, and developed a set of ground rules for the team. We talked about the differences in Mental Maps, and we identified some of the unwritten rules in the organization.

The big milestone occurred after a session about learning to resolve conflict, when the team agreed to hold a session to surface past hurts and conflicts, which I call Unpack Your Sack. Using a script and candy worms to symbolize the past hurts, the team talked through a number of difficult issues, some which members of the team had been holding onto for years. At the end of this session, the team members said they felt as if a weight had been lifted, and they were ready to start fresh with one another.

With all of their work on communication and relationship skills, the team meetings were much more productive. Some people did slide back into old behaviors now and then, but with the other team members holding them accountable for adhering to the ground rules and for using their new skills, the backslide did not last long. Even though most of the focus was on communication and relationship skills in the team meetings, the changes also spilled over into their working relationships outside the meetings. Less than a year later, the company had significantly reduced its backlog problem and was enjoying a profitable year.

The process of setting ground rules, as we did with the management team, is not easy because it involves articulating assumptions that people take for granted. Setting ground rules is a two-part process. First, have the team brainstorm a list of expectations they have for their behavior and the behavior of others. Second, once a list of possibilities is developed, the team needs to agree on the rules and the wording of the rules. It is important that everyone on the team is involved in developing the ground rules, instead of having them imposed by one person.

Teams sometimes resist discussing and setting ground rules because they feel that it takes away from the "real" work of the team, or because they compare the exercise to the old days of being in school and having the rules written on a blackboard. Articulating ground rules may seem a little juvenile and it does take time and energy, but in the end, it saves time and relationships.

Here are a few examples of ground rules from teams I have worked with. Some of the rules might seem obvious, but during the discussions to develop the ground rules, people are always surprised at how differently other people can interpret each area when it is not articulated.

- Anything disclosed in team meetings that could be considered sensitive or confidential in nature should remain within the team.

- Encourage involvement of all team members and balance participation.

- Build trust with each other.

- Practice open communication.

- Choose not to take things personally; realize and accept disagreements. Avoid personal attacks.

- Encourage one another.

- Show respect, courtesy, and value differences of all team members.

- Support team decisions.

- Put hidden agendas on the table.

- Celebrate successes. Have fun. Share food.

CUSTOMER MAPS

Customers have maps of companies and products, while companies have their own maps of customers. Brands are the maps that customers have for a company, product, or service. Profiles composed of demographics and psychographics are the maps companies have of their customers.

Customers buy brands because they are a shortcut. They make the purchasing decision easier by representing a set of expectations. When a customer contemplates a purchase, a brand promises that the experience of the product or service will live up to certain expectations. Brand maps are built through trial, advertising, or word of mouth information.

On the other side of the coin are the maps that companies have of their customers. Sales and marketing professionals develop customer profiles based on certain demographic or psychographic characteristics and these profiles influence how the company thinks of its customers. Profiles determine how a company talks to its customers, and they also affect the products or services that a company offers. Unfortunately, profiles comprised of numerical data provide only a limited picture of customers. Especially in this age of the Web-based lifestyle, these profiles may no longer represent customers in a manner that is helpful to companies in product/service development or marketing. The Internet has made it clear that one 40-year-old-Caucasian-married-with-children-woman-customer is not the twin of another.

For example, Booz-Allen & Hamilton studied the behavior of Internet users and found that customer profiles based on demographics did not predict behavior on the Internet. Instead, the consulting company's study showed "usage-based segments that correlate to users' on-line moods and goals." Based on this information, the company mapped "online occasions" which predicted key behaviors such as shopping. They found that occasion "was a clue to the user's mood, and the mood helped predict behavior—including, notably, the likelihood to go to certain sites, even the propensity to shop." (Rozanski, Bollman, and Lipman, 2001).

To broaden their viewpoint of customers, companies need to think of customers in terms of the customers' lives, not just as a compilation of numbers. That is why storytelling is a powerful tool in helping business people understand their customers. Storytelling helps people see the bigger picture of how their products and services fit into a customer's life. When I work with companies on strategic thinking, one of the exercises I like to do is to have small groups of people choose a picture ripped from a magazine ad or editorial layout and create a story about the customer, based on a list of questions. This exercise helps people use more of their brainpower when they think about customers, which results in new ideas for products and services and new techniques for promoting the company.

ACTION TOOL: Telling Stories

One way to tap into your ideas and insights about customers is to tell stories about customers, services, products, competitors, and so on. Storytelling is one way of identifying your assumptions about your customers, why they do or don't buy your products/services, and how customers use them.

When I work with groups, I take a bunch of photographs and images ripped from different magazines. Then I have small groups of two or three people choose an image and use a list of questions (like the following list I developed for a business products company) to create a story. Change the questions to fit your business.

1. What is the customer's name?
2. Are they male or female?
3. How old?
4. What is their job? With what company?
5. Where do they live? What city and state? Is it a house, condo, or apartment?
6. Do they have a family? Describe.
7. What are the major tasks in their workday?
8. What are their hobbies?
9. What are their hopes? Fears?
10. What keeps them awake at night?
11. What are their favorite movies? Why?
12. What are their pet peeves?
13. Where did they go to school? What degree did they earn?
14. What were their favorite classes?
15. What kind of car do they drive?

Once people have created the story, examine the implications for your business, the products/services you offer to customers, and how you might better serve the customer in your story.

SHIFTING MAPS

Mental Maps are useful tools until that day the world shifts and the maps don't shift with it. For individuals, these shifts include events such as taking a new job, joining a different company, or getting a different boss. For organizations, they include events in the larger world, such as the shifts that are taking place now in the business environment because of forces like technology, globalization, and demographic changes.

In business today, many people are operating from Mental Maps with faulty assumptions. The rules you learned in the industrial economy—whether you learned them from another person or from trial and error—do not work as well in this new world. Many people are trying to navigate the new world with maps that no longer fit the terrain, and they are wondering what went wrong.

The natural reaction to this shift in terrain is to deny that something significant has changed or to believe that, even if something has changed, it won't last, so if you hang in there long enough, things will snap back to the familiar way. Unfortunately, while people are standing in the middle of the road waiting for this reversal to occur, they get whipsawed by the winds of change.

For example, in the old days people navigated using a map that said if you are good at business, you are good at analyzing, compartmentalizing, predicting, and controlling your world. Part of that map included a picture of terrain that looked pretty much the same in front as behind, so you could forecast the future based on past experience. In this new business environment, on the other hand, chaos and unpredictability rule. Interdependent systems mean that one action has unpredicted consequences.

Another predominant map of the old economy was based on the work of Frederick Taylor, who popularized Scientific Management in the early 1900s (see more about Taylor in Chapter 1). Business people learned from Taylor, as well as those who followed in his footsteps, to treat employees like factors of production, just like machines. If I push this button, change this process, or turn the tension knob, I can get the result I want. Today people are learning—particularly if their businesses deal in any kinds of intangibles—that people are not factors of production, and they cannot build a successful business if they treat them like one.

It is important to examine your maps because, when the business environment that a company is operating in shifts, old rules and assumptions can interfere with the company's ability to make the necessary changes to succeed. Take a look at a few of the old and new unwritten rules that I have identified (below) and see if any of the old (expired) rules are lurking in your organization.

Old Rules	*New Rules*
Fear is the best motivator.	Opportunity and challenge are the best motivators.
Fun does not belong in the workplace.	Laughter, fun, and play are essential ingredients for creativity and innovation.
Employers select employees.	Employees select employers.
The pie is limited, must fight for a bigger piece.	Grow the pie.
Perfect your product before you sell.	Use iterative prototyping.
One career for life.	Portfolio of careers.

WE CAN'T DO *THAT*!

Maps also affect an organization's ability to create and innovate. To create and innovate, an organization must be able to recognize, challenge, and sometimes destroy their old maps, and that is not easy to do when they are the maps that have helped the company be successful up until now. To create and innovate, people have to think in different ways, to see new possibilities, sometimes to connect outrageous ideas. Maps can squash new possibilities when they bump up against old assumptions of how things should be.

Maps also affect innovation when they include a prohibition against asking questions, taking risks, or making mistakes. When people are precluded from exploring, they are unlikely to develop new ideas. Companies that have maps that include rules like: "Dot the i's and cross the t's," "Don't rock the boat," or "Don't question what it's not your place to question," shut down new possibilities and new ideas.

One of the most effective tools for encouraging innovation is to identify and challenge maps about your customers, your products, and your industry. What your customers want from you this year is not necessarily what they will value next year. Considering each of the assumptions in your maps, ask yourself, "If this wasn't true, what would we be doing differently?" or "If this changes next year, what do we need to change to be successful?" Companies can also challenge their maps by thinking about the people who are not their customers. Many times innovation happens in the population that you aren't serving. If you challenge your thinking about these customers by asking, "What would we need to change to serve this group?" you may identify some innovative opportunities.

When Jacques Nasser was head of worldwide auto operations for Ford Motor Company, he developed a revolutionary plan to cut costs by challenging the old maps about customers. One of the elements of the plan was to eliminate slow-moving car models and shift that production capacity to models that produced higher profits. Traditionally, automakers don't eliminate car models because past experience has shown that dealers complain, suppliers complain, and market share suffers. So, in Detroit, the industry map includes an unwritten rule that says, "don't eliminate models." Nasser, however, felt the downside would be outweighed by the savings Ford would realize. When Nasser and his team actually talked to the dealers and suppliers about eliminating the slow-moving models, they discovered that the maps they were operating from were no longer valid. In a 1998 *Fortune* magazine article titled "The Gentlemen at Ford Are Kicking Butt," Nasser said: "The interesting part was when we went out to explain to dealers and suppliers why we were doing it. We were losing money and they were losing money on the same products. They were wondering why we were keeping them, and we were keeping them because [we thought] they wanted them." (Taylor, 1998, pp. 73–74)

To bring to the surface the old assumptions and unwritten rules that might be blocking innovation (like "don't eliminate models") I like to do an exercise called "We Can't Do *That!*" when working with groups in brainstorming and strategy sessions. By focusing on the "cannot do's," "do not do's" and the outrageous, we are able to bring to the surface the assumptions and unwritten rules that are blocking innovative ideas. Focusing on the "can't do's" also releases people from feeling the pressure to pluck innovation from thin air. Because it starts with the familiar, it lowers the performance anxiety in a group. It is important when using this exercise, though, to follow the usual rules of brainstorming (no criticism, no idea is bad, and so on), so the group doesn't get off track by evaluating the "can't do's" before they have generated enough ideas.

When we play "We Can't Do *That!*," people are surprised at how often they *could* do something if they consider it from a different perspective. Often the blocks to transforming a can't do into a can do are old, outdated assumptions. When people are given the tools to identify these assumptions, it not only encourages more innovative thinking in the meeting, it also spills over in their working life, because identifying assumptions is top of mind for them.

Another way to nurture innovation in a company is to hold Assumption Days to identify and challenge the assumptions the company is using to operate. On Assumption Days people can challenge products, processes, and policies to see if the assumptions underlying decisions are still valid. A great question to ask on Assumption Day is "If we were starting this company from scratch, would we do this now (or would we do it this way now)?"

Companies can also encourage innovation by making it safe to bring up new ideas. Joel Barker tells a story in his book, *Paradigms: The Business of Discovering the Future*, about one of his corporate clients who lowered the risk of suggesting innovations by creating a Trial Balloon Day. On Trial Balloon Day, people in the company could sign up to present an idea to an evaluation committee. "The committee, schooled in the concept of paradigms and their influence, would listen to the new idea and examine its merits and risks with the innovator. If it was a good idea, the committee, plus the innovator, would carry it up two levels. If the idea was inappropriate, the innovator could leave anonymously." (Barker, 1993, p. 207) The Trial Balloon Day provided the opportunity for suggesting innovation without the risk of embarrassment.

You have probably heard of the concept that the most innovative ideas come from people who are new to a job or on the outside of a business. In some cases, that is true, because people who are new or outsiders are not hampered by maps that keep them from seeing possibilities. However, some of the best innovation is the result of experienced people who pull aside their maps and see their industries, companies, products, and customers with fresh eyes.

KEY POINTS

▮ People rely on Mental Maps, made up of assumptions and unwritten rules, as mental shortcuts.

▮ Mental Maps are similar to the psychological concepts of schemas and scripts. Schemas are people's organized patterns of knowledge about the world. Scripts are a particular type of schema.

▮ Mental Maps, like schemas and scripts, set up expectations about how the world should operate. They also determine the focus of attention.

▮ Maps influence what people see and do not see.

▮ People learn assumptions and unwritten rules from watching others, and from trial and error.

▮ It is important to identify assumptions and unwritten rules in your maps because they affect your ability to change, to make decisions, and to work with people.

▮ Maps make change difficult because people may screen out information that is not congruent with their maps.

▮ Mental Maps are important in decision making and risk taking because maps affect what you pay attention to in a decision situation, the factors you ignore or discount, and your assumptions of cause and effect.

▮ Different maps can cause misunderstandings, conflict, and miscommunication between people.

▮ Conflicts between Baby Boomers and Generation Xers are the result of different Mental Maps.

▮ Articulating expectations, intentions, and purpose help to make your maps clear to others and improves working relationships.

▮ Organizational maps serve as a lens through which the organization sees people, products, customers, and the marketplace.

▮ People in organizations share maps; it is sometimes difficult for them to see outside the boundaries of the organizational map.

▮ Maps provide a decoder for understanding a particular organization's assumptions and unwritten rules.

KEY POINTS *(Continued)*

I Identifying unwritten rules is important for an organization because they can have negative effects on the working environment, and they can blind the organization to shift and change.

I Conflicts between maps can derail an acquisition or merger.

I Developing vision, mission, and value statements is one way that organizations articulate their expectations.

I Articulating expectations is especially important when an organization is struggling through a major change.

I Articulating expectations improves the working relationships of teams.

I Brands are the maps that customers have of companies, products, and services.

I Problems with Mental Maps occur when the environment shifts and maps do not; when that happens, maps can interfere with a company's ability to succeed in the new world.

I Maps squash innovation when old assumptions squash new possibilities.

7

BRAIN OPERATING PRINCIPLE 5: Repetition Required

People need repetition to learn, whether it is a new skill, instructions for a task, or meeting business goals

A beginning singer spends hours practicing the same scales over and over: *la la la la la la la la la*. A young mathematics student stumbles through his multiplication tables: 2×1=2, 2×2=4, 2×3=6. A budding linguist struggles through her fourth attempt at conjugating the Spanish verb to be: *Yo estoy, tu estas, el esta*. What do they all have in common? Learning through repetition.

Repetition is a key part of the learning process. Remember that when you learn something new, your brain is actually building new physical connections between neurons. Repetition—whether it is a concept, a thinking tool, or a physical action—grows and strengthens the connections in your brain. Sometimes it takes several repetitions to build those connections. Each time you repeat, it helps to strengthen the connections, so that after numerous repetitions, what was once difficult becomes easy.

Think of repetition like building a bridge across a lake, one pylon at a time. If you only have one or two pylons, it makes for a long jump between the second pylon and the next shore. That jump requires a lot of energy and preparation, and there is always the chance you won't make the leap. However, if you repeat the hard work of installing pylons all of the way across, the distance from shore to shore is easy to traverse.

The Brain Operating Principle of Repetition Required says that people need repetition to learn, whether it is a new skill, instructions for a task, or meeting business goals. The principle explains why when you try something new, it sometimes doesn't work out the first time. It explains why people need practice to learn. It explains the importance of repeating yourself when you want someone else to understand you or to attach importance to what you are saying. It also explains how repetition can condition people to respond to a particular stimulus.

REPETITIVE LEARNING

Repetition is the key to learning. Remember "practice makes perfect"? That is because the more you repeat (practice), the stronger the connections for your brain. Learning through repetition also applies to things you are not repeating on purpose. If you are consistently repeating a negative thought, for example, you are also teaching yourself that thought.

Athletes, musicians, actors, and other types of performers know that repetition is the key to a great performance. They train by repeating the performance over and over. Sometimes they may break it down into parts and repeat each of those parts. Other times they rehearse the entire performance.

Performers have also learned to use visualization as part of their repetition strategy. Because the brain doesn't know the difference between what is real and what is imagined, visualizing is just like rehearsing. It helps your brain build the neural connections it needs to learn, just as if you were performing in reality. Psychologist Richard Suinn did an experiment with members of the U.S. National Olympic Ski Team that demonstrated the effectiveness of visualization. Half the team used visualization—mentally seeing and skiing the run. The other half practiced normally, without visualization. The group that visualized showed so much improvement that they were the athletes selected to compete by the coach. Peter Fox, a psychologist at the University of Texas at San Antonio, compared the brain maps of people performing physical activities with those who only visualized performing the same activity. The maps of the two groups showed activation of similar areas of the brain.

Learning through repetition applies to learning a new language, mastering a new computer program, getting accustomed to using the Internet, or learning a new business initiative. Each of these requires repetition to build expertise. New challenges that feel intimidating at first can become more comfortable through repeated exposure.

Have you ever tried to learn something new and felt like you would never master it? Perhaps it was a new language, a new sport, or a new computer program. At first, all the elements you had to learn seemed overwhelming. It felt awkward, intimidating, and cumbersome. You may have felt that you were too old to learn something new, or that you would never master the complexities well enough to make it work. But over time, as you practiced, it started to click. The skills that seemed so difficult started to come with ease. Soon, you were wondering why you thought it was so difficult in the first place.

Repetition can teach your brain ideas that aren't positive, as well. When you are repeating negative self-talk, you are also building the connections in your brain that make it easier to believe that negative self-talk. Negative messages are easy to repeat. Sometimes they are messages you heard from your parents or teachers growing up: "You're so clumsy," "You'll never make anything of yourself," or "Why can't you be more like . . .?" Sometimes these messages are ones people create on their own: "I'm a hopeless case" or "I'm terrible at math."

Repeating a negative message over and over makes it more difficult to switch to a positive message, because when you try to switch over, the positive message feels strange and uncomfortable to your brain. Unless you repeat the positive message over and over, the negative message will continue to dominate.

What are you repeating to yourself? Pick a day and jot down the negative things you say about yourself. Sometimes when you start paying attention, that is enough to change your pattern. If you need help breaking your pattern of negative repetition, use the old rubber-band-around-your-wrist trick or keep a log to remind yourself to change to a positive message instead.

REPETITION ALL AROUND

People are surrounded by repetition every day. They are exposed to it in repetitive television, radio, and billboard advertising, they see it in political news stories, and they even hear it in music.

For advertisers, the Repetition Required principle is fundamental. They use it to entice us, persuade us, and sell us. Advertisers know that seeing an advertisement one time won't have the necessary impact. It takes numerous repetitions, or what are called impressions in the ad business, to fulfill the goal of the advertising campaign. Budgets and effectiveness measurements are based, not just on the costs of production, but on the reach and frequency needed to influence the target customers.

Public speakers use the Repetition Required principle. You can see this principle at work frequently in political campaigns. Candidates choose a theme and then repeat it periodically throughout a speech, as well as throughout the campaign. Remember former president George Bush's "Read my lips. No new taxes" or Bill Clinton's "It's the economy, stupid"? The most memorable repetitive phrasing in a speech was that of Martin Luther King's "I Have a Dream." King repeated several phrases during the speech, but the two that most people remember were: "I have a dream" and "Let freedom ring."

The magic number of repetitions to produce a memorable cadence is three. In fact, in the speaking world, the idea of repeating a phrase or repeating parallel phrasing is sometimes called the Rule of Three. The Rule of Three does not require exact repetition, but it does require similar phrasing to produce the cadence and impact. An example of parallel phrasing repeated in triplicate is: "Change your thoughts. Change your mind. Change your life."

People were taught to use the principle of Repetition Required when they wrote papers and essays in school. They were told to repeat ideas in the introduction, the body, and the conclusion. They might also have been taught to start a paragraph with a topic sentence, and then to explain that topic sentence in the rest of the paragraph, basically repeating yourself, but with more detail.

You also experience repetition every day when listening to music. Almost every song has a refrain that ties the verses of the song together. It is the repetitive refrain that you remember first when you learn a song. And the part of the song most people can join in singing, even if they don't know the rest.

REPEAT TO TEACH

Why do you think teachers have students write things like, "I will not run in the hall" or "I will not forget my homework" over and over on a chalkboard or on paper? They do it because they know the repetition will make an impression.

Repetition is the key to teaching others, especially repeated communications. It is a mistake to assume that just because you, as the sender (communicator) say something once, the receivers (listeners) hear and understand you, even if your communication is in writing. Communication requires repetition to be effective.

Think about how many communication messages you are exposed to in a typical day. How many commercials on TV, the radio, or in print? How many e-mail messages? Voice mail messages? Conversations? When you consider all the information people take in each day, it is easy to understand how one message can be lost in the onslaught.

Even when people know that repetition is important, they are reluctant to repeat themselves. Perhaps they are afraid that others will think they aren't paying attention and, therefore, are repeating themselves by accident. Or perhaps they get sick of saying the same thing over and over again. However, they need to overcome that reluctance if they want to get through and make a lasting impression.

Repeating a message does not mean saying exactly the same thing exactly the same way every time. In fact, if you do repeat exactly the same thing, eventually people begin to screen out your communication. Remember the idea of selective attention? Part of that dynamic is that the brain is primed to respond to novel stimulus, so changing the wording of a message can be a factor in getting people to pay attention.

Repetition does mean sticking with the same theme or message. In a political campaign, for example, the campaign will decide on a few themes or messages that the campaign will stand on. These themes and messages are played out in many ways, but the repetition adds up to one coherent picture.

Restating an idea is one way of repeating a message. Restating means finding a slightly different way of communicating your message. Besides response to a novel stimulus, the advantage of restating is that if for any reason the listener did not understand your message the first time, the restatement will help them understand you the second (or third) time. Different expressions of an idea appeal to different people. So, rather than feeling that repeating yourself is wrong, think of it as recognizing people's different experiences and thinking processes.

Another way to repeat without using the same words is to quote someone else. Quotes are great for repetition because they repeat your key points while introducing a slightly different perspective on the message. Quotes also add credibility to your presentation or position, and quotes capture peoples' interest.

You can also repeat yourself by telling a story that relates to your message. Storytelling works well for repetition because it engages the listener's imagination and helps them relate to your message in a different way. Also, stories are more easily remembered by listeners than statements of bare facts.

REPETITIVE CONVERSATIONS

Are you facing a difficult conversation? Gearing up to ask for a raise or demand a specific compensation package in an interview? Readying yourself to make a sale and afraid you might choke on the closing? You will find the Repetition Required principle can make a difficult conversation or request much easier. The secret is to repeat the particular phrase, statement, or request that you want to use. This repetition involves more than just practicing the phrasing, it is also familiarizing your brain with the idea and with the words.

Jennifer was struggling with the start-up of an illustration business. Her stumbling block came each time she was asked by a client to quote a fee for a particular piece of illustration work. "I know that I really need to be charging $500 for a project like this one," she told me, "but each time I talk about my fee, out pops $300 instead." I suggested that Jennifer try the 15× Repetition Technique to accustom her brain to quoting her target fee.

The 15× Repetition Technique involves repeating the key statement 15 times in a row each day for several days. At first, it will feel uncomfortable. But remember, that is just your brain at work, making that physical connections. After a few days of repetition, you will find the words flow more naturally because you've grooved the path for your brain.

Jennifer was skeptical that something so simple would make a difference in quoting her fees. But she was willing to try it out. Once she did, she found that her new fee quote came out of her mouth with ease.

The 15× Repetition Technique also works when dealing with intimidating people. If you work with or around someone who uses intimidating tactics, the repetition technique can help you to develop confidence for your next encounter. Let's say that you have a boss that often enters intimidation mode during meetings. You need to make a request at your next meeting with your boss. Use the 15× Repetition Technique to prepare yourself to make the request. You can also anticipate the follow-up questions your boss might have and prepare responses to those questions using this technique.

The principle of Repetition Required is very effective when addressing those people who don't seem to hear you or who try to guilt you into doing something you don't want to do. All you have to do is to keep repeating the same response over and over. You don't even need to change your words.

For example, if someone keeps asking you to do something that you don't want to do, just use the broken-record technique by saying something like, "Thank you so much for thinking of me. I feel honored that you would want me to serve on the anniversary party committee; however, I must decline. Perhaps Jane would be interested" or "I'm working on other projects at this time." Keep repeating the same thing, no matter what they say.

People have grown up with the idea that if someone asks them a question, they should answer it, but, that is not necessarily so. You can use the repetition technique in situations where you want to avoid answering an unwanted question. In this case, identify a set response to use for situations when you choose not to answer. For example, one man I worked with would just reply, "Interesting question" when someone asked a question he did not want to answer.

If avoiding the question seems strange to you, watch people interviewed by the media. They will often subtly or blatantly answer a question with their own message, which might have very little connection to the point of the question. When I worked in public relations and we were prepping clients to talk to the media, we would help them identify their key messages and then help them practice answers to a variety of questions that included their key messages. We also taught people how to bridge from a question they did not want to answer to a message they preferred to communicate. So, if you want to see how to use this repetitive avoidance technique, watch more television interviews (particularly the hostile ones).

ORGANIZATIONAL REPETITION

In the industrial economy, organizational communication was based on an employee's "need to know." Managers communicated only the information that was deemed absolutely necessary for employees to have in order to carry out their duties. For the most part, the rank and file were trained to do as they were told, with the assumption that workers did not need to know the reasoning to do their jobs effectively.

Today, many companies have yet to shift their viewpoint about communication. They don't recognize the key role that communication plays in helping people work effectively.

One of the mistakes made by organizational leaders in communicating direction, new initiatives, and organizational change is not communicating frequently enough. Remember that the Brain Operating Principle of Repetition Required says that people need repetition to learn, whether it is a new skill, instructions for a task, or meeting business goals. The organizational leaders who are the most effective communicate regularly, and they recognize that communication is especially critical during times of uncertainty and change.

Organizational leaders also need to be aware of the impact of negative conditioning that is the result of repetition. Whether it is conditioning that thwarts change or conditioning that teaches customers to feel annoyed, the effects of negative repetition and conditioning can undermine or block the organization from meeting its goals.

WHY USE REPETITION?

The leadership of an organization teaches through repeated communication. Repetition facilitates learning, directs focus, and demonstrates importance.

CEOs and other senior executives often labor under the mistaken impression that people in the organization hang on every word they say. For a few employees, that may be so. But for the majority of the organization, breaking through requires repetition. A single decree, however carefully worded, does not have the impact or effectiveness of a campaign.

Sometimes managers hesitate to repeat themselves because the task of developing effective communication is difficult. They would prefer to develop one comprehensive message and be done with it. Developing messages and communicating them takes time and energy away from tasks that are perceived as more important.

Managers also resist repeating themselves because they become bored with the message after repeating it several times. Just like advertisers who become bored with their ads long before customers, managers hear their own messages and get tired of saying the same thing. Sometimes managers hesitate to repeat themselves because they don't want to annoy people. Or they won't repeat themselves because they think the onus of understanding is on the listener.

In the case of corporate internal communications, it can also be costly to repeat communications. When the communication needs to reach a large organization and it requires production, duplication, or mailing, repeating the communication can be expensive. Because of the prevailing attitude that a senior executive should only have to communicate once, the cost of repeated communication is difficult to justify. It can be even more difficult to justify the expense when there is a culture of communicating on a need-to-know basis.

Most organizations underinvest in internal communications. They do not allocate the time or the money needed to help employees understand the direction, priorities, and goals of the company. The leadership of an organization will easily invest large blocks of time or significant dollars to make sure that other stakeholders, such as Wall Street analysts or major customers, understand the company's point of view. However, when it comes to employees, many executives will not make the same investments. They either don't see employees as important or they are under the mistaken impression that one, singular communication is all that is needed.

For communication to be effective, however, it needs to be repeated. Employees are exposed to so much information, on and off the job, that for a message to break through the clutter and be understood, it must be repeated several times, sometimes several hundred times. Adrian Slywotsky and David Morrison proclaimed in *How Digital is Your Business?*: "We sometimes say: Communicate your message not once or twice but 700 times. We promise you: The 700th time you make The Speech, use The Slogan, or hammer home The Idea, someone in the room will grasp it for the first time. It's virtually impossible to overrepeat your most important message." (Slywotsky and Morrison, 2000, p. 277)

How can that be? A person may be distracted by other priorities, not feeling well, or just not listening. Even if they "hear" the message early on, it might not make sense to them at that moment. They may need to hear the message at a different time for it to make sense to them in the context of their own particular job.

In addition to using repetition for understanding, you can also use it to direct focus and demonstrate importance. Employees will focus on the things that you repeatedly say or do (whether you intend them to or not). When you want to focus your employees' attention on a particular initiative or area of work, use repetition. When you want to highlight the importance of a message, use repetition. The first time people hear something they may dismiss it as unimportant. The second time, they may not attach any significance to it. However, if they hear the same message again and again, they soon realize that the message is an important one.

Repetition is particularly important in organizations that are prone to frequently shifting priorities. If your organization is one that jumps from one priority to another, employees may become "tone deaf" to announcements of new initiatives. They stop listening because they assume the newest priority will change again next week, so there is no reason to waste their energy listening or implementing. Repetition tells people that you haven't changed your mind about the critical priorities; that you are not a victim of program-of-the-week syndrome.

REPETITION FROM THE TOP

If you were to shadow some of the most successful CEOs on the job, you would find they invest a lot of time and energy in repeated communication to their organizations. Whether it is through speeches, videos, memos, or e-mail, or by integrating the message in other ways, effective leaders recognize the value of repetition.

Jack Welch, former CEO of General Electric, mastered the art of frequent, repetitive communication. Welch used speeches, memos, interviews, e-mail, and so on, to hammer home his message. Welch was also well known for his prolific notes that encouraged, praised, and thanked employees.

Technology makes repetitive communication easier. Tools

like e-mail, intranets, internal portals, and screen savers give leaders and managers accessible, cost-effective channels for constant
communication.

For example, Martin Sorrell, the chairman and CEO of WPP
Group PLC, a global advertising agency, uses e-mail to keep people informed and to share his perspective on trends and issues. Sorrell says,
"Because I need to stay connected to our organization—to let people
know what's on my mind—I write to all of our people once a month
(through e-mail, of course). I talk about how the company is doing, I
discuss a particular issue, I offer my perspective on (say) new business
models for the Internet. . . . it's a great way to let people know what I'm
working on." (Taylor, 1999, p. 236)

Even before technology made communication simpler, Alan
"Ace" Greenberg used regular memos to communicate business policies and remind employees of the firm's business philosophies. In
fact, Greenberg became famous for his humorous memos during his
tenure as chairman of Bear Stearns. One of his techniques was to use
fictional characters, including the colorful Haimchinkel Malintz
Anaynikal and his nephew, Itzhak Nanook Pumpernickanaylian, to
continuously focus employees on basic business essentials like mini-
mizing expenses, returning phone calls, and avoiding complacency.
For example, in a January 1980 memo, reprinted in his book, *Memos
from the Chairman*, Greenberg cautioned employees about complacency by quoting Anaynikal as saying "'thou will do well in com-
merce as long as thou does not believe thine own odor is perfume.'"
(Greenberg, 1996, p. 16)

The importance of repetitive communication was one of the recurring themes in the book, *Lessons from the Top*. Authors Thomas Neff
and James Citrin interviewed 50 top business leaders about their
philosophies, experiences, and strategies. In his interview for the
book, Al Zeien, former chairman and CEO of The Gillette Company,
dubbed his style of communicating as preaching. He said, "I preach a
lot. I'd say 90% of my time is spent on 'the three Ps'—people, product,
and something I call 'purpose,' but it's really preaching. This is explaining to people all the whys. Why do we have to close this plant up? Or
why should we do this? Or why should we do that? That's preaching."
(Neff and Citrin, 1999, p. 348)

Mike Armstrong, chairman and CEO of AT&T Corporation, told

Neff and Citrin how he emphasized repeated communication. Armstrong said, "You've got to give the same speech too many times. You've got to go to the lunch bag forum with discipline. I write an article every month for the company newspaper. I do videotapes. I do company broadcasts. Communicate, communicate, communicate! You cannot be a remote image. You've got to be touched, felt, heard, and believed." (Neff and Citrin, 1999, p. 39)

REPETITION DURING UNCERTAINTY AND CHANGE

Using the Repetition Required principle is particularly important for organizations during times of uncertainty or change. Repetition helps people understand what is changing, comprehend the need for change, and integrate the change into their own working environment. It also helps prevent the negative assumptions that people naturally make when faced with uncertainty.

I have a saying, "Repetition is the mother of understanding." It came in handy when I was working with clients that were implementing a major change in their company because it helped them recognize the importance of investing in repetitive communication. With a strong, traditional, patriarchal culture, the general feeling of the management team was that they only needed to explain the change once (in one memo) and everyone would understand. In their view, one detailed, carefully crafted piece of communication should be sufficient to explain the change.

One piece of communication won't fulfill the goal of communicating, which is to help people understand. When an organization is in transition, implementing a major change (or even a minor one), people can be distracted by all of the uncertainties. They are worrying about what the change means for their jobs, salaries, benefits, careers, or their status in the company. They are not focused on listening to what the leadership team wants them to hear, they are focused on figuring out what the change means to them in terms of their fundamental survival. In times of change and uncertainty, then, it is particularly important to communicate repeatedly.

With the prevailing business viewpoint of organizations as machines, it is difficult for managers to understand that unlike machines, people cannot just change out a part or buy a software update. People are more complex than even the most complicated business machine. When changes are necessary, people need encouragement, the tools to change, and help in using the tools.

As much as leaders might wish that people would change instantly, the reality is that change takes place over time. People need time to absorb new concepts, to think through the effects on their job and to experiment with new ideas and behaviors. That is one reason why it helps to repeat communication over time. As people are experimenting with the change, they are ready to hear different parts of the big picture and to understand what they heard.

When people are learning something new and uncertain, it helps to break communication into parts and repeat those parts. When trying to learn something new, too much information at one time can be overwhelming. If people get overwhelmed, they shut down and stop listening. The technical term for this syndrome in human communication theory is *information overload*. Breaking communication into pieces increases the odds that people will be able to absorb the message. You have probably heard the joke: "How do you eat an elephant? One bite at a time." A big change is like an elephant. It requires judicious carving if it is going to be ingested.

REPETITIVE CONDITIONING

An advanced use of the Repetition Required principle is called *conditioning*. You may not know it, but you probably already use this tool. Is there a certain song that puts a smile on your face? A smell or a food that evokes memories? These are conditioned responses, created through repetition, and made even more powerful when they are linked to an emotion.

Conditioning produces a particular response, built through repetition. A researcher named Robert Zajonc developed a theory in 1968 called the mere exposure theory. The theory says that through repeated exposure to a stimulus, an individual comes to evaluate the stimulus more favorably. In Zajonc's studies, he exposed students to nonsense words—words like afworbu, civrada, nansoma—and to

Chinese characters, men's graduation photographs, and Pakistani music, all unfamiliar to the students. The more frequently a word was pronounced, a character or photograph viewed, or the music heard, the more positively it was evaluated. In other words, repetition conditioned the students to like the words, characters, photographs, and music.

Ivan Pavlov's research with dogs is perhaps the best-known example of conditioning. In the most famous experiment, Pavlov taught his research dogs to salivate at the sound of a bell by repetitively ringing the bell at feeding time. You have used this same mental process in your life when you conditioned yourself to feel good or feel bad, or to evoke a particular memory, by repetitively using music, food, or particular sights or smells.

Parents teach their children to respond to certain tones of voice or certain phrases. When a parent says something like, "I'm not kidding, mister," or starts to count, children know it is time to take them seriously. Parents also condition kids to respond to a particular look or gesture.

A lot of your conditioning is not consciously chosen by you. You form the associations, but you don't do it on purpose. You know when you've made the link between two things, but you don't always remember how that link was formed.

Let's say you are going through a difficult time at work and every morning for several weeks, when you arrive at your office door, you feel a deep sense of dread. Later, even after your outlook toward your job improves, you continue to feel that dread the minute you hit your office door, but you cannot identify what it is that you are dreading. Here is what happened: You conditioned yourself to feel dread. Your office door has become the trigger (like Pavlov's bell) for bad feelings.

The good news is that once you know the secret, you can change that conditioning. Using the same process (deliberately now) that you used before, you can trigger good feelings instead of dread. Triggers work by forming an association between emotions or memories and a particular stimulus—an image, sound, word, taste, smell, and so on. Although triggers normally operate below the screen of the conscious mind, it is possible to identify them by paying attention. You can identify a trigger because it automatically evokes the emotions or the memory. It is a conditioned reflex.

ACTION TOOL: Theme Song

The Theme Song tool shows you how to use conditioning to feel happy, motivated, energetic, or confident whenever you want. To use this action tool, pick a song that will be your conditioning stimulus. Make sure the song has a melody you can sing or hum, and words that have a special meaning for you.

Once you have chosen your theme song, sing or hum the song at least three times a day, and while you are singing or humming, think good thoughts. Think about what makes you feel happy, confident, successful, joyful, powerful, optimistic, grateful, and so on, while you are singing or humming the song. After six weeks of practicing this conditioning, you will be able to trigger those powerful feelings just by singing or humming your theme song.

TRIGGERING OTHERS

Once you understand repetition and conditioning, you can use it with other people—like colleagues and customers—as well as yourself. You can encourage good feelings, incite a sense of urgency, or even lower stress, using conditioned triggers. When you use conditioning with other people, you can either use triggers that have a shared significance or develop your own triggers using repetition.

Triggers with a shared significance are those that have a common meaning among people. Within cultures, companies, or particular groups, there are words, phrases, expressions, or symbols that carry a particular meaning and are recognized for that meaning.

I used my knowledge of conditioning in sending invoices to a frenetically busy client. After one lost invoice that was enclosed in a white envelope, I realized I needed to find a way to make sure that my invoices got noticed when they arrived and were not shuffled into a pile of papers where they could disappear. Because people are conditioned to see red as a color of importance and urgency, I switched to sending the invoices enclosed in red envelopes. The result? No more lost invoices.

I also use my knowledge of conditioning when mailing invoices to other clients. My goal is for clients to feel happy to hear from me, whether they are receiving ideas, information, or an invoice. When I send invoices, I include small packages of candy or an interesting quote on a card.

I heard a story about one smart salesman who used a shared trigger to get past the staunch gatekeepers at one company. His weapon of choice? Chocolate. The salesman would load up his pockets with chocolate in various forms and use it to create goodwill and open doors.

Food, in general, has a lot of emotional significance for people. Many celebrations, societal rituals, and memories of being nurtured are connected with food. Therefore, food has the potential to serve as a powerful shared trigger. In fact, studies by Gregory Razran, a psychologist, found that people became fonder of the people and things they experienced while they were eating. Razran called his studies the "luncheon technique." He theorized that because of the processes of association and conditioning, it was possible to attach the good and favorable feelings evoked by food to anything that was closely associated with good food. So, for example, communication that is presented in conjunction with good food has a greater chance of being heard and viewed favorably.

ORGANIZATIONAL CONDITIONING

The shifts in the business world demand that organizations change if they are to succeed. Unfortunately, many organizations have taught employees not to risk change, and that kind of past conditioning can be a powerful deterrent to change.

The old rules of business emphasized command and control. People were taught to emphasize punishment over reward. A lot of conditioning was directed toward preventing the possibility of making a mistake. The problem with the business philosophy of command and control is that it is fear based. And it has conditioned people who have worked for years in this kind of environment to avoid change because change requires trial and error, and error results in punishment.

In a 1993 article in *Sloan Management Review* called "How Can Organizations Learn Faster? The Challenge of Entering the Green Room," Edgar Schein explained, ". . . avoidance behavior learned through punishment not only is more stable than behavior learned through reward but also does not tell the learner what the correct response is and does not encourage trial and error learning." (Schein, 1993, pp. 19–20)

In other words, conditioning in organizations that is based on punishing mistakes is stronger and longer lasting than conditioning based on rewarding success. It means that organizations that previously focused conditioning on avoiding mistakes cannot suddenly turn about and expect people to become risk takers overnight, no matter what rewards are offered. It also means that companies that have a cultural history of command and control will have a tough time joining the ranks of learning organizations because they have, in effect, reinforced the idea that learning is not a valued behavior. Schein made this point very succinctly in the article when he said, "To the extent that our present managerial theories emphasize the stick over the carrot, we are building in strong resistances to new learning." (Schein, 1993, p. 20)

Companies that decide to initiate a change cannot snap their corporate fingers and expect the ranks to respond. Change requires planning and patience, even when it appears to be a simple matter of retraining. Even a simple change may be more complex than it appears because of past conditioning.

For example, one company that I worked with decided to change their selling strategy and needed to battle old conditioning to do it successfully. Traditionally, the company had relied on advertising and distributors to sell their products, and the company's sales force mainly called on distributors. Therefore, in general, the sales reps only had contact with the end user customer when there was a major problem with a product that the distributor could not resolve alone. In that case, the distributor called in the sales rep.

The company decided it wanted sales reps to begin selling directly to end users, and to switch to a consultative selling approach. The difficulty in making this transition was that the sales reps were conditioned to view the end user customers as difficult, demanding, unreasonable, and so on, because most of their contact with the end user customers came as a result of complex problems that distributors could not handle. The customers at that point of contact were naturally upset, since they had already tried to resolve the problem through the distributors and the distributors had, in turn, called in the sales reps. Therefore, if the new sales strategy was to be successful, the company needed to change the sales force's conditioning about end user customers.

This situation illustrates how past conditioning can erect an invisible wall to change. In this type of situation, an organization cannot just teach people a new skill and expect them to change. The sales reps needed to overcome years of negative conditioning. They needed the opportunity to spend time with the end user customers in a non-threatening environment—one that would allow them to have conversations that weren't about problems with the products. We created a series of future-oriented meetings where sales reps and customers talked about the future of the industry, by developing scenarios and discussing the implications. The meetings provided the chance for sales reps to see customers in a different light (and vice versa), as well as to build relationships outside of the sales process. Only when the reps had that experience were they able to break through those years of conditioning and start putting their new sales skills to use.

REPETITION AND CONDITIONING WITH CUSTOMERS

Organizations can use the Repetition Required principle with customers and clients, as well. Repetition can help customers understand a complex product or service. It can also create favorable or frustrated feelings toward an organization and its products.

Just as teaching employees something new requires repetition over time, introducing customers to a new concept or new product requires repeated communication. It is naive to think that a company can create the one, perfect communication that will make such an overwhelming impression that it won't need repeating. Customers have many demands on their attention, too, so if companies want to break through the clutter around their customers, they need to communicate over time.

Advertising departments recognize the impact of repetition and conditioning. They especially understand the emotional leverage of conditioning. That is why advertisers use celebrity spokespeople, and why they use familiar music that customers associate with happy memories. Consider how many advertisers are now using music from the 1960s, 1970s, and 1980s—music that brings back happy, youthful memories for that large group of consumers known as the Baby Boomers.

Brand image is built through the use of repetition and conditioning. The experiences customers have with a brand, the advertising they see about a brand, and the conversations they have about a brand all combine to create a specific image. If the image is one the customer wants to be associated with, the customer will be predisposed to buy that brand. When experiences, advertising, and conversations are repeated, they can create a compelling link between the pleasurable feelings and the brand. This compelling link, created by the power of repetition and conditioning, is the reason why Philip Morris was asked to stop using the evocative image of the Marlboro Man in advertising for cigarettes.

Companies can condition customers to feel happy or frustrated, based on the contacts customers have with the company over time. When contacts are satisfactory, customers associate pleasant feelings with the company. But when those contacts are discouraging or frustrating, customers associate negative feelings with the company.

Many business people do not realize the conditioning influence of small annoyances over time. In a conversation on this topic with B.J. Farrell, an Orlando-based sales trainer, B.J. and I talked about the insanity of the numerical menus on business phone systems and the frustrating process of trying to get through to a human being who can answer a question or solve a problem. B.J. first described his irritation at having to follow a long, convoluted series of numerical menus. B.J. then expressed his annoyance at the business systems that required him to enter his account number in order to reach a human being, only to be asked to give his account number again once he reached a human being. This is just one example of how companies teach customers to feel frustrated as a result of repeated contacts with the companies.

It is important to recognize that when strong emotions are involved, it does not take very many repetitive contacts for a customer to create that feeling of frustration toward a company. One way organizations can keep from conditioning their customers to feel frustrated is to take an objective look at what it is like to do business with their organization and to change policies, processes, and systems that cause frustration. It is difficult, sometimes, for an organization to put itself in the shoes of its customers, so using mystery shoppers or outside consultants to test the systems and provide feedback is a good way to uncover contact points that are cumbersome or frustrating.

KEY POINTS

I People need repetition to learn, whether it is a new skill, instructions for a task, or meeting business goals.

I Repetition grows and strengthens connections in the brain; people learn through repetition.

I Repeating negative self-talk teaches you to think negatively.

I Repetition is the key to teaching others; communication requires repetition to be effective.

I You can repeat through restating, quotes, or storytelling.

I Use the 15× Repetition Technique to make a difficult conversation or request easier.

I One of the mistakes leaders make in communicating direction, new initiatives, and change is not communicating frequently enough.

I Repetition facilitates learning, directs focus, and demonstrates importance.

I Most organizations underinvest in internal communications.

I Successful business leaders invest a lot of time and energy in repeated communications.

I Repetition is particularly important for organizations during times of uncertainty or change.

I Repetition can produce a conditioned response or reflex.

I Use repetition to trigger good feelings by forming an association between emotions and a particular stimulus.

I Use conditioning to encourage good feelings in others, incite urgency, and get your foot in the door.

I Many organizations have conditioned employees not to risk change.

8

BRAIN OPERATING PRINCIPLE 6: What You Focus On Expands

What people focus on will grow in their perception

From the moment you begin perceiving events or people in a particular way, your mental army goes on maneuvers to back up your hypothesis. Psychologists call this the confirmation bias; the tendency to seek out and interpret information in a way that confirms your original hypothesis or belief.

The principle of What You Focus On Expands says that the questions you ask and what you choose to focus on will determine your experience of the world. Your OSE brain looks for what you tell it to find, and it keeps looking until you tell it to look for something different. What You Focus On Expands because of selective attention. Remember the discussion of selective attention in the chapter on the OSE brain? Daniel Goleman explains how attention is influenced by relevancy:

> What gets through to awareness is what messages have pertinence to whatever mental activity is current. If you are looking for restaurants, you will notice signs for them and not for gas stations; if you are skimming through the newspaper, you will notice those items that you care about. What gets through enters awareness, and only what is useful occupies that mental space. . . . Irrelevant information is only partly analyzed, if just to the point of recognizing its irrelevancy. What is relevant gets fuller processing. For example, if you casually scan a newspaper page and suddenly see your name, it will seem to "leap out" at you. Presumably the words

you saw as you skimmed were partly processed and found irrele-
vant; your name—which is always relevant—rated full process-
ing. [Goleman, 1986, p. 66]

Goleman also explains how a particular focus can dominate a person's attention: "An activated schema dominates awareness; it glides from the pool available and guides attention. As you walk down a street, you may not notice a dog approaching, but the relevant schema for dogs would float toward preconsciousness. At the moment you hear a growl, though, the 'dog'—or perhaps the 'dog bite'—schema becomes the most highly activated, and the dog looms into aware-ness." (Goleman, 1986, p. 84)

You can use the focus principle to help or hinder your effective-ness at work. You can use it to focus on how much you hate your job, the overwhelming nature of your To-Do list, or how much you dislike a certain person. Or you can use the focus principle to help you ac-complish your work and your goals. You can let the focus principle op-erate in your life without conscious direction—letting it run amok and hijack your day—or you can put the principle to work for you.

ATTENTION INFLUENCES PERCEPTION

Each person inhabits a world of their own. To your brain, there is no concrete reality, there is only how you experience your daily world. What you pay attention to makes up your perception of the world.

The What You Focus On Expands principle explains why a person will see so many Honda Accords on the road just after purchasing a new Accord. It explains why you notice laptop computers in the airport when you are contemplating buying a laptop. You see what you want to see or what you are mentally ready to see. You pay attention to data that con-firms your thinking. In other words, you see what you are looking for.

FOCUS ON GOALS

The principle of What You Focus On Expands explains why goals work. When you focus your brain on achieving a particular goal, your brain helps by paying attention to the factors that will help with that goal. For example, when you are focused on attaining a goal, opportunities and ideas appear on your scope. You see possibilities that relate to the goal that you never saw before. Often the opportunities and ideas were present around you, but you were not paying attention to them.

Your brain will help you to achieve a goal if you make that goal your focus. Think of focusing on a goal like creating a bulletin board for your brain. The bulletin board provides a space for your brain to connect ideas together to help with your goal. It also provides boundaries to keep extraneous ideas off your scope so they don't distract you.

You have probably heard that writing down a goal makes it more powerful. Writing down a goal helps your brain reinforce the thought by repeating it (remember the Brain Operating Principle of Repetition Required). If you write down the goal and then review it regularly—by putting it in your wallet, posting it on your bathroom mirror, or putting it in your organizer—it keeps your brain focused on the goal.

You don't even need to be completely sure of the path to reach your goal. If you stay focused on the goal, your brain will find answers to help you along the way. One way to create that path is to ask your brain questions that relate to the goal. When you ask a question, you give your OSE brain instructions to think about the question and to find answers and ideas that relate to the question.

Mike is the owner of a small business. When he bought the business it was struggling financially, but with several years of hard work, Mike turned it into a thriving enterprise. With the business running well, Mike was looking for a new challenge; a new direction to take his business. He knew it would involve adding new products or services, but he wasn't sure what those products or services might be, or how to go about finding them. I recommended that Mike begin by setting a goal of just exploring possibilities. I suggested he read some business-related magazines and make note of ideas that interested him, even if they didn't seem to make sense for his business. I also suggested that he focus on being open to ideas and not worry about having the answer for a month or two.

A few weeks into his exploration, Mike was introduced to another small business owner. As they discussed their businesses, it became clear that an alliance could benefit both businesses. If he hadn't been focused on exploration, Mike probably would not have picked up on the opportunity.

LANGUAGE DETERMINES FOCUS

The language people use, out loud and in their heads, also affects their focus. If you use positive language, your positive outlook expands. When you use negative language, your negative outlook grows.

A positive focus does not necessarily mean pretending that nothing is ever wrong. Instead, it means using more positive language and spending more time focused on the good than the bad. How often is your self-talk positive? Do you self-talk phrases like: "Wow, that was so creative of you," "What a great idea that was," or "You're a genius" or do you tend to self-talk more negative phrases?

Two kinds of language are particularly powerful. One is the use of loaded words. The other is the use of absolutes. Loaded words are those that pack an emotional wallop or create a vivid picture in your mind. Loaded words include those like: dynamic, ecstatic, winner, fascinate, triumph, bombard, reckless, explode, tragedy, horrific, stupid, and devastating. They also include expletives. Pick up a newspaper and you can easily find examples of loaded words because loaded words are powerful for our brains. They push the brain toward a particular focus—positive or negative. Loaded words can also create an emotional response. For example, when you use negative loaded words, you create anxiety and fear. Everyone has some words or phrases that have personal emotional loading because of some experience they've had with the word.

Absolutes are words that represent extremes. They are words like: always, never, all, none, no one, everyone, awesome, horrible. Talking in extremes affects your focus because it limits the choices for your brain. When you instruct your brain using absolutes, you limit the possibility for change. What your brain hears when you use an absolute is that it must be this one way and only this one way.

For most people, negative language comes more naturally than positive. When you beat yourself up with negative self-talk, you will only make more mistakes. Beating yourself up decreases your self-confidence, and the less confident you are, the more prone you are to errors. Also, your brain takes the self-talk and searches for reasons to back it up, and then makes sure those reasons are easily accessible to you, thereby expanding the negative in your thoughts.

The effect of language on focus also applies to the language you hear around you. If your colleagues spend a lot of time complaining about the boss, the customers, or their jobs, those constant negative comments will push you to focus on the negative, as well. Try an experiment during your next meeting. Track how many negative loaded words and absolutes your colleagues use. Then, notice how that negative focus impacts how you feel about your job.

FOCUS AND RELATIONSHIPS

The principle of What You Focus On Expands also impacts working relationships. What you focus on in your relationships with other people can be the cause of conflicts and problems or it can help you find common ground with another person.

Focus is the reason for a lot of fractious relationships and conflict in the workplace. When people get stuck in focusing on the negative, even the most innocent of remarks from another person is viewed with suspicion. Every action is seen as another straw on the camel's back. No matter what the other person does, it is seen as a negative.

This kind of focus on the negative often escalates the conflict between people. The more that people focus on the negative characteristics of another person, the larger the area of conflict grows. Instead of just one point of disagreement, their OSE brains have now identified enough points to construct an entire picture—similar to the way the pixels in a computer graphic create an image.

What do you do when you realize you are nurturing a negative picture of another person? First, recognize that you have to be willing to shift your focus from the negative to the positive. No amount of logical reasoning will change your mind until you make that decision and give those instructions to your OSE brain. Once you make that decision, begin identifying even the smallest of positive characteristics. You can even purposely exaggerate those characteristics in your mind, so they will outweigh your previous negative focus.

FOCUSED LEADERSHIP

The effectiveness of a leader is determined by his or her focus. If a leader is focused on the wrong factors, employees will be focused on the wrong factors. If, for example, a leader is focused on fear, which plays itself out by the leader not taking risks or demanding there are no mistakes, employees will be focused on not making mistakes instead of on producing great work. If a leader is focused on strengths (or what an employee or the organization does well), that is where employees will be focused also.

A common misguided focus is an obsessive attention to mistakes—either a focus on how many mistakes are made or on preventing mistakes. The problem is that when you focus on mistakes, that is what will grow in your perception. You will not see the numerous tasks that are performed correctly or the payoff from creative risks.

For example, during a coaching session, a client complained about the volume of mistakes his employees were making. He asked for advice about whether he should fire those employees and start over or if there was some way to teach people not to make mistakes. It was difficult for me to believe that in a business that was growing successfully, so many critical mistakes were being made. I asked the CEO to try an experiment. For one week, I asked him to focus on catching his employees doing something right or well. After that week, we could reevaluate the idea of replacing staff or finding some new disciplinary technique to control mistakes. It was amazing the difference this little experiment made in his perspective of mistakes—the number of mistakes in the company dropped dramatically.

In many businesses, managers are under the false impression that their job is to prevent mistakes by their employees. They believe that if they create enough policies, procedures, and fear, they can control people to the point that no mistakes will occur. It's a holdover from those days when the business world viewed companies as machines and the job of a manager was to plan and control.

For instance, Max works for the in-house production group of a world-famous entertainment company. As an outsider, you might think this was one of the most creative companies in the world. However, the vice president in charge of his department is focused on fear and control. The vice president, clearly insecure about his abilities and hoping that no one will catch on to his ignorance, is unable to give clear direction to the staff and he berates the staff whenever they present a project that does not meet his unspoken expectations. On top of that, he starts a witch hunt to finger the culprit whenever a staff member makes a mistake—complete with a special meeting to debrief the problem.

The vice president's attitude and behavior has created a department full of stressed and fearful people. Productivity is low because people spend the majority of their time writing memos, creating paper trails, and taking other measures for covering themselves in case a mistake is made.

Effective leaders, on the other hand, focus on the positive instead of the negative. When an employee makes a mistake, they help them learn from it. Effective leaders also know that focusing on the positive tends to reduce mistakes, whereas focusing on mistakes tends to increase them.

A common mistake that is made by executives who take over the leadership of an organization is to focus first on identifying what is wrong and trying to fix it. Meg Whitman, CEO of eBay, has a different perspective. In an interview with *Fast Company* magazine, Whitman said, "People are very proud of what they've created, and it just feels like you are second-guessing them all the time. You are much more successful coming in and finding out what's going right and nurturing that. Along the way, you will find out what's going wrong and fix that." (Fishman, 2001, p. 74)

Focusing on the positive helps to build people's confidence, and when you build confidence, it encourages people to perform better. Effective leaders encourage employees by recognizing the tasks employees do well and by highlighting their strengths instead of their weaknesses. The best boss I ever had focused on her employees' strengths, not their weaknesses. When I was a young 20-something, Margie Cooke told me that one of the secrets to management was to identify the interests and talents of an employee and then shape the job to the employee's interests and talents. Perhaps that was one reason why Margie's employees worked long hours, invested their creative talent, and persevered in the face of adversity.

FOCUS AND CREATIVITY

The principle of What You Focus On Expands is one of the keys to creative thinking. What you pay attention to and the questions that you ask affect your ability to create—whether that creation is an innovative idea or a solution to a problem.

Developing ideas is a result of shifting perspective and making connections. Creative lore says that many inventors developed their ideas by shifting their focus and connecting disparate elements through the use of questions. Bill Bowerman, who invented the airsole unit of Nike shoes, reportedly asked himself "What would happen if I poured rubber into a waffle iron?" Fred Smith, the founder of Federal Express, pondered the feasibility of an express shipping company that borrowed from the hub and spoke model of commercial airlines. And Albert Einstein was said to wonder, "What would a light wave look like if I were riding it?"

You have probably heard the story about how Post-it Notes came to be. The engineer who invented the adhesive for Post-it Notes, Spencer Silver, was actually trying to create a super-strong adhesive. Instead, he created one that would only stick temporarily. Another engineer, Art Fry, suggested the new adhesive could be used for bookmarks, so they wouldn't slip out of the book. Fry also decided to ask a question to widen the focus from bookmarks to other possibilities. He created samples of paper with the weak adhesive, gave them to the secretaries at 3M, and asked them, "What could you use these for?" The rest is history.

Generating ideas can also result from a broadened focus that allows you to scan for inspiration and possibilities. When you broaden your focus, you see things in the environment that you would otherwise miss.

When you are solving problems, the elements you focus on will direct the course of your solution. Because What You Focus On Expands, the parts of the problem that you focus on will appear to be the most important. You've heard the old saying, "To a hammer, everything looks like a nail." The power of focus is that it determines how you perceive things and how you will react.

For example, if you focus on the components of a problem that appear to be impossible to solve, the problem will seem like it has no solution. On the other hand, when you focus on the elements that have an obvious solution, the problem will appear easier to solve. Often the key to solving a problem is simply to shift your perspective and to approach it from another angle, so that you are focusing on different areas of it.

PUTTING FOCUS TO WORK

Focus can help you change—whether that change is a new job or a new perspective on the world—because you determine where to direct your focus.

When you make a decision that you want to change yourself—to change jobs or even to change professions—focus can help you make that change. The secret is to learn to focus on what you can do or to focus only on the next steps, not on the whole big, intimidating picture.

Again and again in working with coaching clients, as well as in talking to other entrepreneurs who have tackled a big venture, I find it is the final vision of the change that inspires. It is also this big picture that intimidates, because when people focus on everything that has to be done to achieve that big change, they feel overwhelmed.

For example, if you decide to explore new job opportunities, and you look down the road at the myriad of scary, unknown, difficult tasks involved, it is overwhelming. You have to figure out what jobs you are qualified for, what jobs you are interested in, you have to write a resume, identify organizations and people to talk to, survive interviews, sell yourself, negotiate, and so on. It is no wonder so many people decide to stay where they are, even if they are unhappy. For major projects, like changing jobs, when people focus on the big picture, they quit before they even get started because of the intimidation factor.

The secret, then, to making those changes, is to focus on a few steps you can take immediately. When you have achieved those steps, then focus on a few more. It's like taking a long journey in a car; you focus on the next stretch of road or the next turn you need to make, not the final destination. So, to explore a new job, the first few steps might be to update your resume, ask a friend for feedback on the new resume, and look into jobs that interest you even if they aren't in your city or in your field. Then focus on how to contact the companies that interest you.

Focus can also help you shift your perspective when you are in a negative place or stuck in a bad attitude. When you are stuck in a negative attitude, use this principle to change what you are paying attention to. Shift your focus and you shift the data coming into your brain. There are several techniques for shifting focus that can help you get unstuck. The first is to focus on what has worked (or is working) rather than what hasn't (or isn't). The second is to shift from focusing on the past to focusing on the present. The third is to expand your focus by putting the situation in a bigger context. The fourth is to change the questions you are asking yourself.

Focusing on what has worked (or is working) can be a challenge when you are stuck in the negative. One of the techniques I use to shift my focus when business is slow, when a project seems impossible, or when something doesn't work out the way I want is to remind myself of past successes. I keep a file called "Yeah, Shannon!" that is packed full of thank-you notes, accolades from clients, and other reminders of my successes. This file gives me a boost and helps me get perspective when I am sliding into a negative focus.

Shifting your focus from the past to the present is a useful technique when you are too focused on things that have gone wrong in the past. The key to shifting to the present is to tell your brain this is a different time, to emphasize that you are not repeating the past. You can point your brain toward a focus on the present by asking questions such as "How is this situation different from the past?" or "What can I do to make the outcome of this situation different?"

The third technique is to expand your focus by putting the situation in a bigger context. A bigger context means recognizing that this is just one incident in a lifetime. Or telling yourself, as the popular saying goes, "It's not brain surgery." One way to put the situation in a bigger context is to ask yourself: "Will this be important to me in five years?"

The last technique for shifting focus—changing the questions you are asking yourself—can also be used in conjunction with the other three techniques. Changing the questions you are asking might include shifting from asking yourself a question like, "Why does this always happen to me?" to asking questions like, "How could I prevent this from happening to me again?" or "What could I learn from this experience?"

ORGANIZATIONAL FOCUS

Several years ago I was on a shoot for a television ad and had the pleasure of watching a very talented director plan each image for a sequence of shots. It was fascinating to watch the process of his work. He would often use his fingers—joined together to form a shape similar to a picture frame—to screen out extraneous visuals and focus on the image that he felt would express the message of the

---

ACTION TOOL: The Ritual Shift

The Ritual Shift action tool helps you get unstuck from a negative focus. It is not unusual for individuals or groups of people to get stuck in a negative focus, and when you are stuck, it is difficult to make the shift. Using The Ritual Shift is easy. Just pick a ritual and perform it. It can last a few minutes or a few hours, depending on your preference. Your ritual can be anything that has a symbolic meaning for you. However, for a ritual to transform your thinking, it requires three important elements:

1. Use at least one tangible object in a symbolic way.
2. Hold your intention in mind as you perform your ritual.
3. Pay attention to the ritual as you are performing it.

Suggestions for rituals to shift a negative focus include:

❚ Write down your negative thoughts and bury them.
❚ Write down your negative thoughts and burn them.
❚ Have a birthday party.
❚ Have a funeral.
❚ Transfer your negative thoughts to a tree or plant.
❚ Write down your thoughts and put them in a box.

---

commercial. The director knew that to get the results he wanted, he had to choose a focus.

Choosing a focus is important for organizations as well. The principle of What You Focus On Expands, applied to an organization, says that the questions the organization asks and what the organization chooses to focus on will determine the operating behavior and viewpoint of its people.

What a group or organization focuses on is mainly determined by the leadership. The priorities that are emphasized, the behavior that is condoned, the actions that are rewarded, and the questions that are asked, all play a part in determining an organization's focus. These focus cues have a powerful impact on an organization's ability to implement projects, its innovation potential, its capacity for change, and its relationships with customers.

STRATEGY AND FOCUS

Business strategy is all about focus. When an organization develops a business strategy, it is choosing where to invest its resources, which include time, attention, and money. It is choosing a desired focus. Business people have built a lot of mystique around the processes of developing a winning strategy, whether those processes are scribbled ideas on a restaurant napkin or closed-door creative sessions. Strategic thinking is an important skill in business, but it is only one step on the path to success.

It's one thing to choose a focus by developing a strategy; it's another to actually implement the strategy and achieve that focus. Strategy is only an organization's desired focus. Implementation (achieving the desired focus) is one of the most difficult, most complex tasks in business today.

Ram Charan and Geoffrey Colvin studied several dozen CEO failures and concluded that in most cases, it is bad execution instead of bad strategy that accounts for failure. In a 1999 article on "Why CEOs Fail" in *Fortune* magazine, Charan and Colvin said, "In the majority of cases—we estimate 70%—the real problem isn't the high-concept boners the boffins love to talk about. It's bad execution. As simple as that: not getting things done, being indecisive, not delivering on commitments." (Charan and Colvin, 1999, p. 68)

Execution requires that the people of the organization understand the strategy and the path to get there. It requires that the organization is directed toward that strategic goal. The most effective way to direct the focus of an organization is to articulate expectations and then to reward people when they meet those expectations. Articulating expectations means communicating the business strategy, and then outlining the critical skills and behaviors needed to implement the strategy. It is a simple concept to grasp but much more complex to implement.

There are three basic reasons why many leaders fail to articulate expectations:

I Leaders assume that once they have voiced the strategy, it is up to other people to figure out how to get there.

I With too much time and energy invested in developing the strategy, there is no energy left for articulating expectations.

I It is just plain hard work. Particularly in this business environment of uncertainty, it is very difficult to define expectations because there are so many variables. A leader may be able to define the outcome or result they want, but the path to reach that goal eludes them.

Focus is determined by what is rewarded and what is discouraged in an organization. When the real reward system is in conflict with the stated goals of the organization, attention will be directed toward those behaviors that are encouraged and away from those that are discouraged. For example, if a person working in an inbound customer service center is told to provide great service to each customer, but he or she is rewarded for completing a specific number of calls each hour, providing great service is not what they will focus on. Another example can be seen when an organization rewards making the numbers, even if it means managing people in an abusive manner or cutting corners.

In some organizations, leaders do articulate the expectations and the reward system is based on the desired behaviors. If a leader is clear about what he or she expects, and the reward system clearly outlines those expectations, there is no conflict for employees in fulfilling those expectations.

For instance, Carlos Giraldo is the owner and CEO of Central Reservation Service, a hotel reservation service. Carlos is brilliant at defining the numbers that make the financial aspect of the business successful. But he also believes there are aspects to learning and development, building relationships with customers, and building relationships with colleagues that are important for his employees to focus on. To help the managers in his business pay attention to these elements, Carlos has them fill out a simple monthly report, called "How Am I Doing?" The monthly report focuses on four areas: goals, improving business knowledge, increasing the business network, and giving praise and thanks.

The monthly report includes these questions:

HOW AM I DOING?

Goals I set last month for myself.

1.

2.

3.

Give yourself 10 points for each goal met.   _____

How I improved my business knowledge.

List how you have improved your business acumen either through reading (specify what), self-training on programming skills, or other business-related study courses. *Give yourself 1 point for each hour you've spent in enhancing your business knowledge.*

_____   _____

_____

How I increased my business network.

List how many contacts you have made with hotels, customers, or other people that can help you in performing your job. *Give yourself 10 points for each new contact you've made this month and corresponded with by either e-mail, fax, or "snail" mail.*

_____   _____

_____

_____

How many people I praised and thanked this past month.

List the people you have praised and thanked by either e-mail or written note this month who are either a colleague, a subordinate, a hotel contact, a customer, or a company vendor. *Give yourself 10 points for each instance.*

_____   _____

_____

_____

FOCUS ON MEASUREMENTS

Sometimes companies become so focused on measurements and numbers that they lose sight of more important things. The business world is enamored with measurement and numbers, and for the most part, these factors will outweigh any others, but a focus on measurement and numbers can lead to a decrease in quality, lost opportunities for innovation, and loss of commitment and motivation of people.

The business world likes numbers because they are controllable, easy to manipulate, and because they fit in a tidy formula. They are much easier to deal with than fuzzy, ambiguous concepts like quality, innovation, and people-centered policies. In the past, most companies were manufacturers of tangible products. The majority of the people hired by these manufacturers were paid to use their hands and not their heads, thus focusing on numbers worked well. Numbers also fit nicely with the prevailing viewpoint that organizations were machine-like, and a manager's job was to control the machine.

Focusing on costs is also popular because you can see a direct correlation between cost cutting and the bottom line. It doesn't take strategic thinking to change the short-term profitability of a company if all you do is cut costs. The problem with focusing on costs is that it doesn't take into account the indirect and longer-term effects on the business. Another problem with focusing on numbers is that it usually results in customers losing out. When there is too much focus on cost cutting, lean inventories, cheaper production, or not investing in innovation, the factors that customers value get pushed aside. Even when customers are price conscious, they still want quality, availability, innovative products, and good service.

For example, a veteran telephone company employee told me about a new policy the phone company had created, which he felt was hurting the installers' abilities to provide good service to customers. The policy evaluated phone installers based on number of installations, without considering the complexity of the situation, so a fairly simple installation that might require 20 minutes received the same credit as a complex installation that might require four hours. Because of the policy, many of the installers began to cut corners on complex installations. As the installers cut corners, more problems arose with the customers' telephone systems, which required installers to return to the site of the original installation to make repairs, sometimes repeatedly.

It is easy to understand how this kind of policy was created. If you only approach it from a direct, simplified perspective, judging productivity based on the number of installations makes sense. But it fails to take into account the larger system, and it also fails to consider the impact on the customer when their phone lines don't work and they have to call for repairs over and over.

Whether you call it downsizing, rightsizing, or capsizing, the end result of the corporate cost cutting of the last two decades is the same: Companies eventually learn that a focus on cost cutting is inherently a short-term strategy. It does make the stock price escalate temporarily, however, it is a strategy you can use only a limited number of times before either running out of places to cut or decimating an organization.

Perhaps the most extreme and colorful example of this lesson comes from the downfall of Al Dunlap, also known as "Chainsaw," during his tenure at Sunbeam. Dunlap was, for a period of time, hailed as the champion of cost cutting and downsizing. He was brought into a business to slash costs and fire people, which increased short-term profits for shareholders. In fact, Dunlap advocated a single-minded focus on shareholder wealth, publicly stating that the only stakeholders in a public company were its investors. Dunlap joined Sunbeam in 1996, and almost immediately shut down or sold two-thirds of Sunbeam's 18 plants, in addition to cutting almost half of its 12,000 employees. Wall Street hailed Dunlap as a hero when the stock shot up. Over the following year and a half, the stock continued to climb.

Then in 1999, the real story began to emerge. It turned out that the financial results the company was reporting were based on aggressive sales tactics and accounting practices that inflated revenues and profits. Sunbeam's investors profited from short-term gains produced by Dunlap's slash-and-burn tactics, but the company itself and its long-term investors paid the price for those short-term gains in the loss of employees, employee morale, customers, and brand equity. Dunlap was fired in July of 1999.

The cost cutting craze taught business executives that in the end, you cannot cut your way to growth. Cutting is much easier than growth because growth requires that you create new value—a strategic move—whereas cutting only requires identifying targets to slash. Cutting is a short-term tactic, whereas growth takes longer-term strategy.

Too much focus on numbers also squelches innovation in organizations. Companies that run only by the numbers tend to squeeze the life out of a new idea before it ever gets legs under it. Ideas that are put through the wringer—prove it, justify it, guarantee it—rarely survive with any semblance of their original creative energy.

It is difficult for an organization that is focused on numbers to see the benefits of innovation, in part because true innovation requires a leap of faith. The benefits may not be evident until the innovation has been implemented or produced and the marketplace has time to adjust.

Focusing on numbers also leads organizations to think of people as costs (a liability), not as assets that appreciate and provide a return. The proof that people really do have an impact on business results is beginning to surface. For example, in its Spring 2001 issue, *The Gallup Management Journal (GMJ)* reported the results of a national survey on worker engagement: *GMJ* found that highly engaged people correlated with higher business outcomes. Other studies have shown similar results—the relationship between employee satisfaction or employee effectiveness and financial results is strong.

INTERNAL AND EXTERNAL FOCUS

One of the common focus problems in companies is focusing internally instead of externally. Focusing inward, sometimes called navelgazing, causes companies to lose sight of their customers' needs. The symptoms of internal focus include putting processes before customers, investing a lot of time on internal presentations, and paying attention to *what* is accomplished, instead of *how* work is performed.

Putting processes before customers is a particular characteristic of large companies, as well as those with a scientific or technical heritage. These companies become so infatuated with creating, documenting, and following processes, that there is no time or energy left for listening to customers. In this corporate environment, when people spend most of their time perfecting the processes, it is easy for them to miss a shift in the marketplace that makes their current business design obsolete.

Too much focus on perfecting the process means little focus on accomplishing important business goals. For example, one of my clients is a big, global company with a scientific and engineering heritage. In this company, process received much more attention than progress. They had very lengthy processes for a number of tasks, including their annual planning, which could stretch well into the year they were planning for. In one case, I was asked to develop the plan for the area in which I was consulting. I developed the plan and submitted it in the format requested. I was then asked to revise the plan, so I did and submitted it. Next I was asked to reformat the same information into a completely different format. Just to put the icing on the cake, two weeks later I was asked, once again, to resubmit the same information in another, different format.

When a company is more concerned about the format of the plan or about presenting the plan than they are about implementing it, they are stuck in a focus on process. When Jack Welch and Lou Gerstner became the CEOs of GE and IBM, respectively, they were concerned with their organizations' preoccupation with internal reports and presentations. Jack Welch was frustrated with the number of reports he was required to generate when he was working his way up in GE. When he became CEO, he reduced the number of internal reports to help the organization become less internally focused. Lou Gerstner viewed the emphasis on creating and making elaborate overhead presentations for internal audiences as one of the symptoms of IBM's loss of focus. Gerstner felt that staff time could be invested more profitably elsewhere, and that elaborate overhead presentations encouraged people to spend too much time in discussion and not enough in decision making. He banished overhead projectors from internal meetings, and encouraged people to communicate prior to meetings so that the time spent in groups could focus on decision making, instead of simply sharing information. Obviously, in any company, some focus should be on perfecting internal processes. The problem comes when the pendulum swings too far in favor of focusing on process. This is usually a symptom of trying to control people, of fearing that if you don't spell out the process in minute detail and keep your eye on it every minute, someone will make a wrong move.

Another internal focus that hurts companies happens when people pay too much attention to winning internal battles, thereby missing opportunities to win in the marketplace. Competitive energy can be a great motivator, but internal competition can be more harmful than helpful. When one person or one division of a company can only win at the expense of another, eventually the company itself begins to lose out. It is more productive for a company to turn that competitive spirit toward external competitors, providing colleagues with a common enemy to fight. The common enemy might be a competitor or it might be obsolescence. When colleagues work together against a common enemy, competitive energy is focused on helping the company succeed, not on fighting with each other.

The idea of using internal competition to motivate and improve performance is based on old maps, created during the industrial economy. In the 1920s studies showed workers produced more when they were competing against each other than when they were not, but this higher output was also associated with poorer quality. However, during the 1920s, quality was not a major concern of most companies, and the workers who were studied were performing repetitive, routine tasks. In fact, studies in today's workplace prove that individual and group performance is usually higher when people cooperate with one another rather than compete against each other. Studies by Peter Blau of Columbia University and Dr. Robert Helmreich of the University of Texas, among others, show that internal competition lowers performance.

Internal focus also shows up as technology for technology's sake instead of the benefits the technology can bring to customers. This is a common tendency in Web-site development. Web-site developers get caught up in what the technology can do, instead of how it functions to benefit customers. The most technically sophisticated solution isn't necessarily the one that provides the best functionality for customers. Sometimes when more technical sophistication is built into a site, it creates difficulty for customers, such as delays in loading pages, difficult navigation, or confusion.

Yahoo! recognized this tendency in the competition between search engines. While other search engines were investing in developing programs that returned more and more sites in each search, Yahoo! decided to focus on how well searches were serving customers, by measuring the number of useful, relevant hits, instead of simply measuring the quantity of sites identified.

Focusing on *how* you accomplish your objectives, instead of just *what* (the quantity) you accomplish is a sign of strong customer focus. In this economy, there is no denying that knowledge work is a larger part of the business equation. What this means is that it isn't just what you do, but how you do it that determines business success. How

ACTION TOOL: Corporate Myopia

Corporate Myopia helps you gauge the strength of internal focus in your organization. To use the Corporate Myopia action tool, answer each of the following questions "true" or "false" based on the majority of people in your organization.

1. We cannot name the top 10 reasons why customers buy from us. ____

2. We cannot name the top 10 reasons why customers don't buy from us. ____

3. Except for salespeople and people in the call centers, most people have not talked to customers in the last five days. ____

4. Most people spend less than 50 percent of their time talking to or about customers. ____

5. There is disagreement in the organization about who is the real customer. ____

6. If you were in your customer's shoes, you would buy from your competitor. ____

7. More than 50 percent of conversations are about internal processes. ____

8. Performance reviews don't include the word *customer*. ____

9. We don't want our customers to talk to each other. ____

10. We don't know what we do that drives customers crazy. ____

11. Accounting has the last word on procedures that affect customers. ____

12. We don't know the major challenges our customers face. ____

13. We don't know what changes our customers anticipate in the next two years. ____

14. It is difficult for customers to complain to us. ____

15. We cannot name the top 10 customer complaints. ____

16. We have never assembled one of our own products, as if we were customers. ____

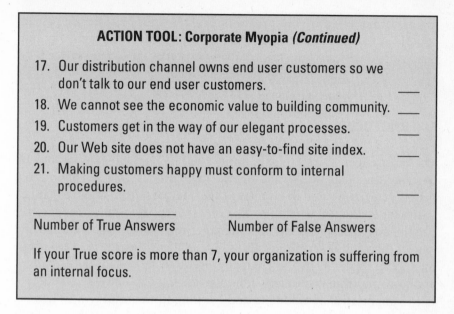

ACTION TOOL: Corporate Myopia *(Continued)*

17. Our distribution channel owns end user customers so we
    don't talk to our end user customers.   ____

18. We cannot see the economic value to building community. ____

19. Customers get in the way of our elegant processes.   ____

20. Our Web site does not have an easy-to-find site index.   ____

21. Making customers happy must conform to internal
    procedures.   ____

Number of True Answers	Number of False Answers

If your True score is more than 7, your organization is suffering from
an internal focus.

instead of what means that instead of counting up the numbers, you
pay more attention to how work is performed, how customers are
treated, and how well a service meets the needs of your customers.

An associate in the CNL Group Inc., a real estate investment
company, captured this idea in one simple, profound statement. Zamena Khan said, "I treat each customer as if they were the first call of
the day." The first call of the day is a simple, but powerful representation of focusing on the *how*. Zamena recognizes that CNL's customers
don't care about the number of calls she has taken that day, the number of requests for information she must process, or what other projects are on her To-Do list. Customers care about getting what they
need and having their problems solved. So, Zamena doesn't just count
up the calls she takes each day (the what), she focuses on *how* she
treats each caller.

Focusing on the *how* is not just about quality control. It is also
about understanding what is important to your customers. Management By Objectives, which is still influential in the management thinking of many companies, taught business people to set and measure
internally focused objectives. These objectives may be important to the
functioning of the company, but they rarely include the elements of the
tasks that create value for customers. Internal productivity, which

might be measured by the number of calls a customer service person completes in a given time frame, may be important to the company, but customers don't care how many calls a particular customer service person completes, just how the calls are handled.

SHIFTING FOCUS

The most effective way to shift an internal focus to an external one is to spend time listening to and interacting with customers. That means people at all levels and in all roles in the company need to have regular customer contact. It used to be that only salespeople, customer service people, and market researchers included regular customer contact as part of their job descriptions. But today, in a customer-driven environment, every person in the company needs to be watching, listening, and learning from customers. John Chambers, CEO of Cisco, believes in the importance of talking to and learning from customers. Whether it is in the form of a phone call, a personal visit, a strategy session or a speech, Chambers invests 80 percent of his time talking with customers, and he expects every Cisco executive to spend 50 percent of their time talking with and learning from customers, face to face.

In their book, *How Digital Is Your Business?*, Adrian Slywotsky and David Morrison noted that companies on the leading edge of leveraging digital design in business were much more external in their viewpoint. "The typical executive of a digital company is outside his or her office 80 percent of the time, talking to customers, suppliers, distributors, and investors, watching the markets move, and searching for patterns of change. Other employees learn to think that way as well. They continually ask: What's next? What's out there? When and how will we have to change again?" (Slywotsky and Morrison, 2000, p. 293)

In this economy, even hourly wage employees can add value to their jobs and their companies by understanding more about how customers use products and services in the context of everyday lives and jobs. Some companies go so far as to have employees work side by side with customers for a day or a week to understand the customer's point of view. Putting themselves in a customer's shoes also helps provide an emotional motivation for focusing on quality factors. During a plane trip, I got into a discussion with the marketing director of a furniture company. He described to me the impact of having people inside the company put themselves in a customer's shoes. To help them understand what it was like to be a customer of their company, they had an unpacked crate of furniture brought into an empty space, and then gave a team of employees the assignment of unpacking and assembling the furniture. When the employees experienced frustration firsthand, with things like missing pieces and directions that were not clear, it was infinitely more powerful than any secondhand statement or market research about customer satisfaction.

FOCUS ON CUSTOMER RELATIONSHIPS

Companies that are externally focused also focus on building long-term relationships with customers. They are more likely to invest time and expertise in core clients, not just in trolling for new clients.

How much do you invest in building relationships with your current customers? How does that stack up against your investments in advertising and marketing? When I say investments, I am not just referring to money. I am also referring to the time and creative energy your organization invests in current customers.

There is an economic value in investing in your customers; in focusing on keeping your customers. Reducing customer attrition, by providing the service and products that clients value, can be very profitable for companies. In fact, the University of Pennsylvania's Wharton School of Business did a multi-industry study that showed companies who reduce their customer attrition by just five to ten percent increase their profits by an average 25 to 75 percent.

When a company is focused on getting new customers, and that is what gets rewarded, people in the company often lose touch with the needs of existing customers. Remember the long-distance telephone wars, when MCI, Sprint, and AT&T battled to convince you to switch your long-distance telephone service? Did the battle win new customers for the companies? Yes. But it also had the unfortunate consequence of teaching customers to constantly switch around for the best deal. And it taught existing customers that companies did not value their continued business. In addition to teaching customers to constantly switch around, the companies also lost the ability to focus on what would keep customers happy—details like improving service, investigating customers' future needs and how the company could meet those needs, or developing new products. When a company is too focused on constantly acquiring new customers, it doesn't have resources to invest in taking care of current customers.

FOCUS AND CHANGE

An organization's focus can also determine its ability to change and innovate. Organizations that recognize small changes and those that reward risk taking (even when it means making mistakes) create an environment that nurtures innovation and change. On the other hand, when people are focused on scoring big wins only, when they fear the penalties of failure, or when an organization lets critics run amok, it shuts down innovation and hinders change.

Again and again it has been shown that companies that nurture an innovation mentality are more successful if they listen and reward even the smallest new ideas. These companies implement suggestions by employees even if they do not have a clear linear payback, as long as the suggestions are not overly expensive or potentially harmful. When people see their ideas are taken seriously, they start to voice more ideas, and the more ideas they voice, the more ideas they have. The result of this focus on ideas—both big and small—is a bias toward innovation.

Businesses that focus only on rewarding success, and those that punish failure, lose the ability to innovate, change, or grow, particularly in this constantly evolving economy. In an organization that punishes failure, few people in the company will be willing to take the risks necessary to bring about real change: the risk to voice new ideas, to create new products, to undertake new initiatives, or to experiment.

Many professionals know firsthand how critics can take over a new idea and decimate it. One reason is that it is much easier to criticize than it is to create. Another reason is that people look smarter by criticizing than by agreeing with someone else's ideas. Also critics are rarely asked to prove their criticism, whereas people with new ideas have to prove their ideas will work.

In some organizations, critics are even celebrated and admired. They are given a status reserved in other organizations for those who create or implement great ideas. In these organizations, innovation is rare, because it is easier to find someone to volunteer to criticize an idea than to find someone who will volunteer to champion it.

When an organization's focus is on negative criticism, few people have the courage to take the risk of broaching new ideas. After all, who wants to stand up and paint a red-and-white target on their creative product? It is difficult enough to take risks without knowing in advance that you are likely to be shot down with gusto.

KEY POINTS

I What people focus on will grow in their perception.

I The questions you ask and what you choose to focus on will determine your experience of the world.

I When you focus your brain on a specific goal, your brain helps you by paying attention to factors that will help with your goal.

I The language people use affects their focus.

I What you focus on in relationships can be the cause of conflict and problems or it can help you find common ground.

I The effectiveness of a leader is determined by his or her focus; a common misguided focus is obsessive attention to mistakes.

I What you pay attention to and the questions you ask affect your ability to create, innovate, and solve problems.

I During major changes, focusing on a big picture can be overwhelming; the secret to change is to focus on a few, next steps.

I When you are stuck in the negative, shift focus by considering what is working, looking at the present, changing your questions, or putting the situation in a bigger context.

I Business strategy is a choice of desired focus.

I The success of a business strategy is dependent on implementation, which requires organizational leaders to direct focus by articulating expectations and rewarding people who meet expectations.

(Continued)

KEY POINTS *(Continued)*

I Too much focus on measurements and numbers can lead to a decrease in quality, lost opportunities, and diminished commitment and motivation.

I Too much internal focus causes companies to lose sight of customer needs.

I Shift internal focus by listening to and interacting with customers.

I There is economic value in focusing on customer relationships and retention.

I Focus determines a company's ability to change and innovate.

I Focusing on criticism discourages new ideas and risk taking.

9

BRAIN OPERATING PRINCIPLE 7: What You Resist Persists

When people give their attention to something or push against something by resisting it, that something will persist

Have you ever tried to hold an inflatable rubber ball under water? What happens? The bigger the ball, the more you have to push to keep it under water. And if you don't want the ball to pop up, you have to keep exerting pressure.

Attempting to keep an inflatable rubber ball under water is a great metaphor for the principle of What You Resist Persists. The principle says that when you give your attention to something or push against something by resisting it, that something will persist.

What You Resist Persists because most resistance involves some kind of negative emotion, such as fear or anxiety, and these negative emotions reinforce what you are trying to resist. Evolutionary psychologists believe that our brains are primed to respond to stimuli if it is perceived as a possible threat. In fact, psychiatrist Marti Horowitz has shown that anxiety impinges on awareness. He calls it "intrusion," which refers to "unbidden ideas and pangs of feeling which are difficult to dispel." Horowitz developed a list of different types of intrusion, including "persistent thoughts and feelings, emotions or ideas which the person cannot stop once they start." (Goleman, 1986, p. 45)

People often think of resistance as pulling away, not pushing away, which makes the persistence part of the principle difficult to understand. Why would something persist if you were pulling away? However, if you think of resistance as push (keeping the rubber ball under water) instead of pull, then Newton's law, which predicts the equal and opposite reaction, also explains the persistence.

The principle of What You Resist Persists is the most perplexing of the seven Brain Operating Principles in this book. I think that is because the result of resistance is an indirect, sometimes obscure, reaction that is not visibly and directly connected to the action (of resistance). Cause and effect are much easier to demonstrate with the other six principles, because it is more direct.

It is especially difficult to recognize when the principle of What You Resist Persists is operating in organizations, because of that indirect relationship between cause and effect. However, once you learn the characteristics and warning signs, it becomes much easier to identify.

RESISTING WHAT YOU DON'T WANT

When you resist what you don't want, it shows up again and again. Whether you are resisting making a mistake, a particular emotion, an unpleasant task, or missing a deadline, resisting doesn't make it go away.

For example, trying too hard not to make mistakes causes you to make more mistakes. You know how this principle works if you've ever had to give a presentation and were very worried you would make a mistake. Resisting mistakes makes you tense, causing you to think less clearly. When you become tense and do not think clearly, you are more prone to making mistakes. In making a presentation, the stress of trying not to make a mistake may cause you to say something you didn't mean to say, stumble over a phrase, or forget part of your presentation.

Victor Frankl, psychiatrist and creator of Logotherapy, called the phenomenon of creating what you are afraid of "anticipatory anxiety." In *Man's Search for Meaning*, Frankl explained: "It is characteristic of this fear that it produces precisely that of which the patient is afraid. An individual, for example, who is afraid of blushing when he enters a large room and faces many people will actually be more prone to blush under these circumstances. In this context, one might amend the saying 'The wish is father to the thought' to 'The fear is the mother of the event.'" (Frankl, 1985, p. 145)

Here is another example of What You Resist Persists that happens during presentations: In every audience, there seems to be at least one person who looks unhappy, uncomfortable, or just plain bored. Maybe it is your boss, who is scowling, or an important client who looks like they cannot wait for you to finish. As a speaker, you try not to look at those people and instead, to focus on the friendly faces and those that look engaged. But when you try very hard *not* to look at that unfriendly or bored face, your eyes return again and again to that very spot.

What You Resist Persists is particularly true when you resist an emotion, because that emotion will continue to surface until you acknowledge the information your brain is trying to convey. You might have experienced the persistence of an emotion if you ever tried very hard not to cry in a difficult work situation. The harder you try not to, the more the tears persist. Or, perhaps you were trying to push down the emotion of anger. When you push down anger, it does not go away. It will continue to surface days, weeks, or even months later.

Yet another example of this principle is when you resist an unpleasant task. When you resist an unpleasant task, both the task and the unpleasantness will persist. Unless you make the decision to take action and do something about the task or to change your attitude about the task, the situation will continue to be unpleasant. Perhaps you have to talk to irate customers day after day, and you resist it. In this situation, you have a choice to either change the task or change your attitude.

You may think that you cannot change the task because it is part of your job. Most people assume that if something is officially part of their job, it cannot be changed. This assumption is left over from the old rules of the business world. However, you may find that if you take action instead of just continuing to resist the task, the situation will change. By taking the risk to talk to your boss about the task and your feelings about it, you may be able to change your work responsibilities. You may also be able to help your company to change the processes or policies that are frustrating customers. It is possible that your company does not realize the cause or extent of the frustration. By talking to your boss about the situation, you can be part of a solution for yourself and for the company.

If you cannot change the task, your other choice in this situation is to change your attitude toward the task. Changing your attitude isn't easy, but if you lower your anxiety instead of resisting the task, you may find the task is not as unpleasant. Emotions are contagious and are communicated through the voice, so each time you pick up that phone with stress and resentment, you are increasing the customer's level of frustration on the other end of the phone, because they are responding to your stress and resentment. Also, focusing on the negative expands your negative view of the situation (remember the principle of What You Focus On Expands).

RESISTANT DENIAL

Maybe you think you will outsmart your brain by denying what you are resisting. Unfortunately, denial will just drive what you are resisting underground, into your subconscious mind, where your OSE brain will continue to give it attention.

Denial is a common form of resistance, but when you deny something, you actually give it attention and energy. Every time you push that thing away, you give it the attention you are trying to deny it. In essence, each time you deny something, you recreate it through the attention your brain gives it in the process of denial.

Some people are under the mistaken impression that by denying something, they are controlling it. Actually, the reverse is true. When you deny something, it is controlling you, because giving something resistant attention means that it has a hold on your brain. It is as if you turned your back, trying to pretend something wasn't there, but you had to keep turning around again and again to say, "Go away, leave me alone."

Resistance in the form of denial may be partly conscious and partly subconscious. In fact, a lot of people have a difficult time recognizing that they are resisting, because of the subconscious component. Sometimes resistance in the form of denial results in selective blindness. For example, there may be a pattern of behavior that a person doesn't acknowledge but that is obvious to others. This was the case with Stacey, who came to me for coaching when she was out of work. Stacey had just quit her job as a project manager for a telecommunications company. After going through five jobs and two businesses in the past ten years, Stacey decided that this time would be different. This time she would work with a coach to figure out what she should be doing with her life. Stacey reasoned that if she were in the "right" job, she wouldn't suffer from the same problems that had plagued her on the job in the past.

As Stacey provided more details about her work history, a pattern began to emerge. "I quit because my boss was unreasonable." "I was let go because my boss didn't understand my style of working." "I left because my boss never gave me any feedback." "I was in business twice, but my business partners always let me down." Do you see the pattern? Stacey was in denial about her responsibility in each of these situations.

A coach can help identify the blind spots in a person's thinking that may be causing problems. In Stacey's case, I asked her a series of questions about those past work situations to draw out specific examples of the generalities of being misunderstood and being let down. As she answered my questions, it became clear that her resistance to taking responsibility for herself and her actions was a major problem for her; one that would continue to block her success unless she changed her thinking.

RESISTANT PROCRASTINATION

Resistant procrastination occurs when you resist doing something you know you need to do, like working on a project, answering e-mail messages, or having a conversation with someone. However, as anyone who has ever procrastinated knows, just because you put off doing something doesn't mean it disappears.

It is not just tasks or work projects that people resist and, therefore, procrastinate in doing. They also resist handling difficult relationship issues, such as:

- Asking someone for advice on a work situation.
- Resolving a conflict between themselves and another person.
- Telling someone what they need to do their job effectively.
- Making a request that they think might be refused.

When you procrastinate, whether you are resisting a task or a relationship issue, the thing you are procrastinating in doing persists by maintaining a hold on your attention and your energy. Consciously or subconsciously you keep thinking about it. In thinking about it, you feel the emotions of guilt, fear, or anxiety associated with not following through. Because of those emotions, the resistance of procrastination also causes a lot of stress.

Another form of resistant procrastination is self-sabotage, when someone sabotages his or her own happiness, success, or relationships. People self-sabotage in a variety of ways, including the sabotage of not meeting commitments.

Fear is one reason that people sabotage themselves. They are afraid of failing, being rejected, or looking foolish. One of my clients, Marsha, was sabotaging her happiness and success by pro-crastinating because she was afraid of rejection. Marsha, a manager in an insurance company, came to me because she was very unhappy and stressed in her job. Once we had identified the tasks she en-joyed, the skills she offered, and her life goals, Marsha started the process of job hunting. She developed a resume, drafted a cover let-ter, and began researching potential companies. Marsha was enthusi-astic about the job-hunting process as long as she was taking low-risk steps, like research and preparation. But when it came to actually sending her resume, or posting it on a job-related Web site, Marsha's fear got in her way.

For over a month, Marsha experienced an unusual number of deadlines and crises that prevented her from sending out her resume. A project at work required her to work evenings and weekends. Her friend had a personal crisis that Marsha had to help her through and so on. During that time, Marsha missed applying for several good job op-portunities. She kept telling me that she really wanted a new job, but too many other priorities kept her busy.

When I recognized her resistance I recommended that she divide the task into chunks. One chunk was to commit to sending her resume to one company. Another was to post her resume on one job site. When that didn't work, I suggested that Marsha stop trying for a while, until her life settled down. Instead, I asked her to take 10 minutes each day for the next two weeks to visualize and write a short story about a potential job opening, her letter applying for the job, and the boss's positive response. Each day, the story would be about a different poten-tial boss. Marsha didn't make it through the whole two weeks before her resistance disappeared. She posted her resume on a couple of online job sites, responded to several ads, and went on a series of interviews. Within two months, Marsha accepted an offer for a job that fit every one of her goals and preferences.

See Chapter 4 for more tools for breaking through procrastination.

WHAT ARE YOU RESISTING?

Want to know what you are resisting? What's persisting? Pay attention to your automatic reactions, to what pushes your buttons, to the conflict you experience with others, and to what worries you.

Your automatic reactions are one good clue to what you are resisting. If you automatically react when someone makes a suggestion about one of your projects, you might be resisting having anyone learn that you don't feel completely confident in what you are doing. If you automatically react when someone tells you to do something, you might be resisting someone else's control. If you automatically react when someone brings up a new idea, you might be resisting change. Automatic reactions also include the reactions you have when someone pushes your buttons or hits a hot button. These buttons are emotional reactions to a particular phrase, a specific action, or a certain situation.

Hot buttons are individual, but the hot buttons that affect people at work include:

I Someone who interrupts you when you are talking.

I People who whine.

I Unnecessary processes or paperwork.

I Useless meetings.

I Irresponsibility.

I People who are always negative.

I Deadlines or projects that are constantly changing.

I People who brag.

I Someone who takes credit for your ideas.

One way to identify your own hot buttons is to notice when you use phrases like these:

❙ It drives me crazy.

❙ If it happens one more time.

❙ How dare he/she treat me like that.

❙ I can't stand it.

❙ No one does that to me.

❙ Don't even think about it.

In her book, *Thinking in the Future Tense*, anthropologist Jennifer James recommends another way to identify your hot buttons: "Pay attention when you get a visceral hit—that is, when your stomach jumps—at work, reading the paper, at home, talking to someone, whenever. Catch it, write it down, check it out." (James, 1996, p. 46)

How do hot buttons, the things you are resisting, persist? As long as you are resisting them, you will continue to pay attention to them, and to react to them. When you decide to stop resisting, you will not notice them happening and you will stop reacting. For example, I have a hot button about people who drop names. When someone I am talking with starts dropping names, I can feel myself tense up and stop listening. So when I am resisting name-dropping, it causes me to react. When I stop resisting it, I don't even notice when someone is dropping names.

Another clue to what you resist is your recurring conflicts. If a particular type of conflict occurs frequently, it may be related to something you resist. Your worries are the third clue to what you resist. If you worry about something, you are giving your attention to it by resisting its occurrence. For example, if you are worried about losing your job, you will pay particular attention to other people who lose their jobs, downsizing statistics, the small mistake you made last week, or the rumors about a layoff circulating through your company (as you will recall, What You Focus On Expands).

ACTION TOOL: The Yield Sign

The Yield Sign action tool helps you recognize that you are resisting, identify what you are resisting, and tame the resistance.

Part One: Recognize That You Are Resisting

You know that you are resisting when you:

I Stay in your comfort zone instead of taking a risk.

I Argue instead of listening.

I Avoid feedback instead of trying to understand it.

I Withhold ideas or information instead of openly sharing them.

I Pretend that you know something instead of asking questions.

I Defend an old belief instead of exploring a new one.

I Insist that you are right instead of asking "What if?"

I Assume you have the answer instead of asking a question.

I Protect yourself instead of doing something that might make you vulnerable.

I Blame someone else instead of acknowledging your role in the situation.

Part Two: Identify What You Are Resisting

Use the following questions (or your own) to identify your area of resistance:

I What am I afraid of or worried about in this situation?

I What is the worst thing that could happen here?

I Why do I feel compelled to _____?

I What could I be resisting here?

I What feels like a sore tooth?

Part Three: Give In or Let Go

Use Victor Frankl's paradoxical intention technique by trying to do what you fear. Or, acknowledge the problem by writing it down in a journal.

ORGANIZATIONAL RESISTANCE

Just like resistance by an individual, what an organization resists persists. Resistance in an organization takes time and energy away from other priorities, and it causes organizations to miss out on opportunities created by shifts in the marketplace. When a company resists a trend or shift in the marketplace, it creates reaction from competitors. They may be current competitors or start-up companies that see an opportunity in another company's resistance.

Peter Senge, author of *The Fifth Discipline* and *The Dance of Change*, explains how the principle of What You Resist Persists plays out in organizations. Senge says, "The harder you push, the harder the system pushes back," which illustrates how resistance generates persistence in a system. Senge continues, "Systems thinking has a name for this phenomenon: 'Compensating feedback': when well-intentioned interventions call forth responses from the system that offset the benefits of the intervention. We all know what it feels like to be facing compensating feedback—the harder you push, the harder the system pushes back; the more effort you expend trying to improve matters, the more effort seems to be required." (Senge, 1994, p. 58)

Every organization that I have encountered has at least one issue that it is resisting. Think of the issue like an elephant in the hallway. Everyone knows it is there, but no one confronts it directly. People skirt around the elephant, they avert their eyes, or they hope fervently that it will have magically disappeared one day when they arrive at the office. Still others are in denial, pretending that the elephant is just a part of the decorating scheme. The elephant in the hallway might be a person who is untouchable politically but who causes problems in the organization, an unwritten rule or policy, a problem with an important product or service, a shift in customer needs, a trend in the business environment, or an unorthodox competitor.

Resistance in organizations occurs in a number of different forms. In some cases, it is the entire organization that resists something, and in other situations, it is one group of people within an organization that resists.

RESISTING THE PEOPLE THING

One of the common resistances in organizations is resistance to what I call the people thing. There are two dimensions to resisting the people thing: resisting the fact that people are now a critical part of business success; and resisting the fact that conflict, ambiguities, and emotions are part of human relationships and must be dealt with. When the biggest factors in the business equation (numbers, production lines, machine parts, and so on) were logical and controllable, business was a lot easier. But today, the people thing is a big part of the business equation, and people don't always operate in a logical, controllable manner. Therefore, organizations that are used to command and control find it difficult to deal with the people thing.

Resisting conflict is one way that organizations resist the people thing. It is left over from the industrial economy, when people did as they were told. Organizations don't recognize that conflict is a natural part of human relationships. When conflict is suppressed, it just goes underground and surfaces later as passive-aggressive behavior or as other dysfunctional behaviors.

Organizations also resist emotions. Emotions can be messy, uncontrollable, and sometimes unpleasant. These characteristics conflict with the Taylor-influenced expectation to predict and control, therefore, emotions and their expression are unwelcome in the workplace. What organizations that resist emotions don't realize is that commitment, loyalty, and motivation are all emotion based. There is no such thing as logical or rational motivation, loyalty, or commitment. When organizations discourage people from feeling or expressing emotions at work, they are discouraging people from feeling the so-called good emotions as well as the so-called bad ones.

One reason that organizations resist the people thing is that they don't recognize the economic payoff from treating people as human beings. Numerous studies have shown the benefits organizations derive from people-oriented business practices. For example:

■ "The Ritz-Carlton hotel and resort company finds a direct correlation between its programs of self-directed employee work teams and its increase in guest satisfaction." (Thaye, 1999, p. 1)

❙ "Northern-Telecom's reviews reveal that satisfied employees will serve customers better and have a direct bearing on the company's financial results." (Thaye, 1999, p. 1)

❙ "Among 702 large firms in many different industries, being one standard deviation better on an index of high-commitment human resources practices resulted in an increase in share-holder wealth of $41,000 per employee, according to a study by Mark Huselid of Rutgers University and Brian Becker of SUNY-Buffalo." (Pfeffer, 1998, p. 23)

❙ "Motor-vehicle manufacturing firms implementing flexible pro-duction processes and associated practices for managing people enjoyed 47 percent better quality and 43 percent better produc-tivity than firms relying on traditional mass-production ap-proaches, according to a world-wide study by Wharton School's John Paul MacDuffie." (Pfeffer, 1998, p. 23)

FORMS OF ORGANIZATIONAL RESISTANCE

Resistance by an organization can be a resistance to change in the external environment. When the environment shifts, organizations respond by clinging to the past. They invoke tradition, cite core competencies, affirm their faith in a cherished product, or refuse to invalidate past investments. When resistance to change in organiza-tions takes the form of adhering to tradition, organizations can as-sume an almost belligerent stance toward the push for change. This kind of resistance results in people who recite the history and proud traditions of the organization, and who use tradition to prove why the organization should not change or why a particular change might work for another organization but is not appropriate for their own organization.

Sometimes organizational resistance appears in the form of cling-ing to core competencies. Threatened by the change, people in the or-ganization point to the core competencies as a defense against the change: "We can't do *that* . . . because our core competency is in *this*." When organizations cling to core competencies, what they are resisting is a need to change the business model necessitated by a shift in the market environment.

Clinging to a core competency cost Domino's Pizza a large slice of its market share. Domino's grew to a powerhouse national brand by delivering pizza to college campuses and military bases. Tom Monaghan, founder of Domino's, was adamant that the company stick to its core product—pizza—and one business proposition, pizza delivered in 30 minutes or three dollars off. The company reaped the rewards as pizza delivery became part of the weekly menu in many households. However, when the pizza-dependent boomers grew up and started families, they wanted dinner, not just pizza. Pizza Hut started delivering a broader menu in the 1980s and soon grabbed 50 percent of the marketplace. Domino's continued to lose market share until the organization recognized that its core competency could no longer sustain the company in a changing environment.

There is no denying that core competencies are important, but they aren't an effective defense against change. Especially when the core competency becomes an industry standard, or when it is a competency that the market no longer needs or values. There was a point in time when a core competency in stereo turntable technology was valuable; but no matter how good a company is at turntable technology today, the market is no longer interested. The same goes for manual typewriters, buggy whips, vinyl records, black-and-white TV, and so on.

Resistance to change by an organization can also take the form of what Senge calls "affirming faith in a cherished product." Senge explains:

> *Many companies experience compensating feedback when one of their products suddenly starts to lose its attractiveness in the market. They push for more aggressive marketing; that's what always worked in the past, isn't it? They spend more on advertising, and drop the price; these methods may bring customers back temporarily, but they also draw money away from the company, so it cuts corners to compensate. The quality of its service (say, its delivery speed or care in inspection) starts to decline. In the long run, the more fervently the company markets, the more customers it loses. [Senge, 1994, p. 59]*

Another way that organizations exhibit resistance is in their reluctance to write off past investments. For example, a company will resist change that necessitates an investment in new technology because it requires replacing existing technology, and that current technology may not have fulfilled its projected return on investment. Even if the business strategy clearly demands technology that will enable the organization to interact with customers via the Web or to run software that requires computing power beyond the capability of the current systems, companies are reluctant to write off those past investments.

Resisting change also assumes the guise of simply reorganizing. It is easier to reorganize—to rearrange the deck chairs on the Titanic, as it is often called—than to wade into the risky and unknown territory of changing a business model. So, instead of acknowledging the problems and tackling the solutions, the organization resists and creates instead the illusion that the reorganization will magically solve its problems.

Reorganization as resistance to change is not unique to this uncertain business world. It has been going on for thousands of years, with the same result. Writer and statesman Petronius Arbiter recognized this phenomenon in 66 A.D., when he said: "I was to learn later in life that we tend to meet any new situation by reorganizing; and a wonderful method it can be for creating an illusion of progress while producing confusion, inefficiency, and demoralization."

Resisting by reorganizing might not be new, but the need for frequent and radical change, particularly changes in business design, is a new requirement for survival in this shapeshifting environment. However, frequent and radical change is difficult, so many organizations resist it.

In a *Fortune* article, titled "The Most Valuable Quality in a Manager," writer Geoffrey Colvin outlines the consequences of resisting difficult change. Colvin writes of an "extraordinary 18-month period in 1992–93" when "the CEOs of General Motors, IBM, Westinghouse, American Express, and Kodak—icons of American business—got fired" because of their resistance to changing business models. (Colvin, 1997, p. 280) Colvin also declares, "In a time of revolution, business people must always be prepared to change their business design—the very basis of how they create value or, as we used to put it, make money." (Colvin, 1997, p. 280) He cites the arguments of Adrian Slywotzky and David Morrison of Management Decisions (authors of several best-selling business books), who speculate that in this new business environment, business models may have to change as often as every five years. Slywotzky and Morrison point to the example of Intel's radical change in switching from producing memories to producing processors (see Chapter 5).

THE RESULT OF RESISTING CHANGE

Companies that resist change usually feel the compensating feedback (reaction) Peter Senge talked about, especially when the change is the result of major shifts in the business environment. The push against forces of change creates a reaction in the form of missed opportunities, competitors that snatch market share, and sometimes even obsolescence.

Sometimes companies resist change because the learning curve looks too steep. Especially in today's shapeshifting economy, a shift may mean learning a whole new area of business. The learning curve for leveraging the Internet is especially intimidating, because the technology is new and still changing. Integrating the Internet into a business is like learning to walk as a toddler. It requires perseverance, experimentation, the ability to fall down and get back up again, and the endurance of painful bumps and bruises.

As frustrating and uncertain as the Internet is, companies cannot afford to ignore it and the opportunities it provides. It is one of those forces that is energetically pushing back on companies that resist the changes it is imposing. An article in *Business 2.0*, titled "Are You Next?" talked about the effect of the Internet on industries that are being transformed, or even destroyed, because of the Internet. The resistance of car dealers is one example outlined in the article:

> *Mike Kinnear, owner of a small car dealership in Jasper, Texas, has looked into online referral services, and has his own Web site for prospective customers. But when it comes right down to it, he insists, the Internet is no way to sell cars. "Internet car buying is a fad," he drawls. "We've got a Web site, but as far as selling cars, it hasn't sold the first one." To some, Kinnear's sentiment is good, old-fashioned business sense. To others, it's evidence of a serious epidemic of denial spreading throughout the network of auto dealerships around the United States. "There are a lot of dealers out here who aren't taking the Internet seriously," says Mark Lorimer, CEO of Autobytel.com, which charges the 2,700 dealers in its network a monthly subscription, regardless of how many customers it sends their way. "In terms of getting it, that's clearly necessary. Otherwise, you're in trouble. You become a dinosaur." [Marks, 1999, p. 51]*

One clue that a company is resisting is when it makes derogatory comments about a trend, like those of Kinnear's. This is particularly true when the comments are directed toward a company that the organization is afraid to recognize as a legitimate competitor, usually because recognition would require the resisting company to make significant changes in its business model or business strategy.

Technology is not the only trend that causes companies to resist. Other trends, such as changes in demographics, food trends, changes in the workforce, and shifts in how customers use their leisure time, all provide an opportunity for a company to resist. But resistance doesn't mean the trend reverses, disappears, or that it doesn't have an impact on the resisting company.

Schwinn is one company that suffered because it resisted changing its business strategy to respond to trends. Schwinn was the number-one manufacturer of bikes in the United States from the 1950s through the 1970s. Unfortunately, Schwinn resisted three major trends that developed in its marketplace: motocross, mountain biking, and upscale bikes for adults. The three-for-three record of resistance resulted in bankruptcy for Schwinn in 1992.

Even in a company that is resisting a trend, there are often individuals, or pockets of individuals, who understand the importance of the trend to the business. These visionaries try to communicate the vision and urgency to the rest of the company, but they can get tired of banging their heads against the door. The problem is that at the point a visionary identifies the trend and understands its implications for the business, the trend is still fuzzy, and the importance can only be illustrated by anecdotal evidence that is too easy for management to discount.

At Microsoft, there were three such visionaries who helped to overcome the company's resistance to the Internet. In 1993, when the Internet was gaining momentum as a business tool, Microsoft was growing rapidly, working feverishly to keep up with the demands for Windows. The Internet was not even on Microsoft's scope. In fact, in a *Business Week* article titled "Inside Microsoft: The Untold Story of How the Internet Forced Bill Gates to Reverse Course," Bill Gates was quoted on Microsoft's view of the Internet at that time, " 'I wouldn't say it was clear it was going to explode over the next couple of years,' says Chairman William H. Gates III. 'If you'd asked me then if most TV ads will have URLs [Web addresses] in them, I would have laughed.' " (Rebello, 1996, p. 56)

Three visionaries played a key role in breaking through Microsoft's resistance to the Internet: J. Allard, a newcomer to the company; Steven Sinofsky, Gates's technical assistant; and Ben Slivka, who eventually became the project leader for the development of Internet Explorer, Microsoft's Internet browser.

It was the combination of Allard's and Sinofsky's passion for the Internet that finally got the attention of Gates. Even then, the company dragged its heels, and while Microsoft resisted, the trend persisted, in the form of innovations by competitors, such as Sun Microsystems, Oracle, IBM, Netscape, Yahoo, and Lycos.

In 1995, Slivka wrote a memo, titled "The Web Is the Next Platform," warning that the World Wide Web could make Windows obsolete. The *Business Week* article relates, "At one point, Slivka proposed that Microsoft give away some software on the Net, as Netscape was doing. Gates, he recalls, 'called me a communist.'" (Rebello, 1996, p. 56)

It was not until the fall of 1995 that Microsoft finally stopped resisting and started taking the Internet seriously. *Business Week* noted that "Some 20 million people were surfing the Net without using Microsoft software. Worse, the Web—with a boost from Sun Microsystems' Java programming language—was emerging as a new 'platform' to challenge Windows' hegemony on the PC." (Rebello, 1996, p. 56) Goldman Sachs & Co. even moved Microsoft's stock from its "recommended for purchase" list because of the growing Internet competition.

In response, Microsoft started working full speed on an Internet strategy. In December of 1995, Gates announced to the world that the company would develop a browser, Web servers, and a new Web-based Microsoft Network.

The *Business Week* article declared ". . . Gates has done what few executives have dared. He has taken a thriving, $8 billion, 20,000-employee company and done a massive about-face." The article quoted Jeffrey Katzenberg of DreamWorks SKG, one of Microsoft's joint-venture partners: "'I can't think of one corporation that has had this kind of success and after 20 years, just stopped and decided to reinvent itself from the ground up.'" (Rebello, 1996, p. 57)

Sometimes early visionaries—like Microsoft's Allard, Sinofsky, and Slivka—feel so strongly about the importance of a trend that they start so-called below-the-radar projects, with the hope that the project will provide proof to help sell the idea. At some point, when the trend is strong enough to catch the attention of management, the experimental project helps to break through the company's resistance to change.

The transformation of IBM into a leader in e-business was jump-started by just such a project. The visionary at IBM was John Patrick, one of the company's senior strategy executives. Like Allard, Sinofsky, and Slivka, Patrick's initial tool was a manifesto, called "Get Connected," that turned into a below-the-radar project. When his white paper generated a flood of responses from IBMers, Patrick started a Get Connected mailing list, which turned into a team. The team was unofficial and virtual, linking people in different divisions across the world. Patrick recalled in an article in *Fast Company*, " 'We had no budget, no head count, no authority. . . . Everything we did was informal.' " (Ransdell, 1997, p. 182)

EMPLOYEE RESISTANCE

In some cases, the resistance to change is not at the top. Instead, it is resistance by employees. When organizational leaders make changes, employees naturally resist, especially when those changes are radical and frequent. Resistance to change is a natural reaction. In an article on change in *Fast Company*, Charles Fishman says: "Like a law of corporate physics, people in organizations have an instinctive reaction to the news that someone is going to 'change them': resistance." (Fishman, 1997, p. 64)

Employees resist change for many different reasons. In their book, *Sacred Cows Make the Best Burgers*, Robert Kriegel and David Brandt outline four motives for resistance: "fear, feeling powerless, inertia, and absence of self-interest." (Kriegel and Brandt, 1996, p. 195) Kriegel and Brandt believe that each of these motives must be addressed for organizational changes to succeed.

Just because employees resist a change does not mean they are wrong in their resistance. They may have a legitimate desire to protect the company from what they believe is a serious mistake. Sometimes employees have insights or information about customers that the rest of the company does not have, and their resistance may be based on that information.

Employees also resist because they fear the changes will threaten their freedom. Jack Brehm's psychological reactance theory says that people tend to protect their sense of freedom, so when it is threatened, they attempt to restore their freedom. Although people can be influenced to conform to social norms (remember Solomon Asch's experiments on groupthink and conformity), when the pressure is so strong that it threatens people's sense of freedom, they resist.

Managers sometimes create more employee resistance by resisting the resistance. When employees resist, managers push harder (thinking that force will overcome the resistance), thereby increasing anxiety and fear. When managers push harder, people may consent publicly just to get away from the pressure, but continue to resist privately. Senge says: "When our initial efforts fail to produce lasting improvement, we 'push harder'—faithful . . . to the creed that hard work will overcome all obstacles, all the while blinding ourselves to how we are contributing to the obstacle ourselves." (Senge, 1994, pp. 59–60)

TAMING RESISTANCE

How do you overcome what you are resisting? It seems counterintuitive, but the way to do it is to acknowledge what you are resisting, to give in, or even to do the opposite.

Psychiatrist Victor Frankl created a technique he called "paradoxical intention" to help his patients with problems created by resistance. Remember his concept of anticipatory anxiety, creating what you are afraid of? In paradoxical intention, you try to do or wish for the exact thing that you fear (what you are resisting). Frankl theorized, "in the same way that fear brings to pass what one is afraid of, likewise a forced intention makes impossible what one forcibly wishes." (Frankl, 1985, p. 145)

To use paradoxical intention, try to do the opposite of what you want or move in the direction of what you fear. If you are afraid that your voice will shake when you make a presentation, you could use paradoxical intention by trying to make your voice shake as much as possible. You will likely find your voice won't shake at all.

Frankl advises that a sense of humor is helpful in using paradoxical intention. Humor is especially important when using the technique to take a behavior to the extreme. For example, if you are resisting completing a project because you are afraid that your work won't be good enough, that your boss will chastise you, and that your colleagues will ridicule you, visualize the extreme of what you fear. Make up a story about that situation, and challenge yourself to make it as awful, embarrassing, and ridiculous as possible. You might even think of the story as a cartoon, to make it extreme (and funny).

Sometimes just acknowledging a problem can take care of the resistance and its symptoms. This works especially well when you are experiencing non-specific anxiety because you are resisting a problem. Non-specific anxiety occurs when you feel anxious, but the anxiety is not linked to a specific cause. In this situation, you are pushing a problem away by pretending it doesn't exist, but your subconscious knows that it does exist, so the anxiety persists. When you feel that non-specific anxiety, sit down and mentally dig through the issues in your life. When you hit the one that makes your stomach clench, you have probably identified the source of that non-specific anxiety. Acknowledge the issue and the anxiety often disappears. You don't have to solve the issue or even like it, just acknowledge that it is there, instead of pretending that it is not.

Another technique for dealing with resistance is to give in or let go. Stop trying to do the thing you are resisting, just as I told Marsha to stop trying to send out resumes. When you give yourself permission to give in or let go, the resistance disappears. Then, you can start over, without the resistance blocking you from moving forward.

Organizations, too, can overcome resistance by acknowledging it. Listening to the resistors, acknowledging their concerns, and getting them involved in finding solutions works especially well for organizations dealing with resistance.

Listening is a powerful tool. Sometimes just asking people about their concerns and listening to their responses can decrease the resistance. Mike, the CEO of a marketing firm, found this out when I recommended he use the listening technique with a very vocal employee resistor. The employee was resisting the changes Mike had requested about how projects were tracked throughout the production process, and this employee was making sure that everyone in the company was aware of her opinion. Mike sat down with the employee and asked her to share her concerns. Following their conversation, the employee stopped openly criticizing the new system, and even made several helpful suggestions for improving it.

Getting resistors involved in problem solving is one of the most effective tools for overcoming organizational resistance. Employee resistors can bring a lot of knowledge and experience to the solution. Being involved in the solution also helps to decrease the perceived threat to a person's sense of freedom, thus lessening the potential for psychological reactance. And, as my colleague and former DuPont client, Dale Darling, is fond of saying: "What people are in on, they're not down on."

KEY POINTS

I When you give attention to something, or push against something by resisting it, that something will persist.

I When you resist, you create what you are afraid of; if you are resisting mistakes, you will make more mistakes.

I When you resist emotions, they continue to surface until acknowledged.

I Denial drives what you are resisting underground, where your brain continues to give it attention.

I Resistance in the form of denial can result in selective blindness.

I Resisting can result in procrastination, which causes stress and drains your attention and energy.

I Identify what you are resisting by paying attention to what pushes your buttons, your recurring conflicts, and what worries you.

I Resistance in an organization takes time and energy away from other priorities and causes organizations to miss opportunities.

I The harder you push, the harder the system pushes back.

I A common resistance in organizations is resistance to the people thing.

(Continued)

KEY POINTS *(Continued)*

I Resistance by an organization can be resistance to change in the external environment; organizations often respond by clinging to the past.

I A clue that resistance is operating is evident when people make derogatory comments about a trend or competitor.

I Even in organizations that are resisting trends, there are pockets of individuals who try to communicate the vision and urgency; visionaries play a role in breaking through organizational resistance.

I Resistance to organizational change by employees is natural; sometimes managers resist the resistance, creating even more problems.

I Resistance is not necessarily wrong; sometimes it arises from legitimate concern and a desire to protect the organization.

I Resistance to change may be the result of a perceived threat to freedom.

I To overcome resistance, acknowledge, give in, or do the opposite.

I Listening to resistance, acknowledging concerns, and getting resistors involved in problem solving helps organizations lessen resistance.

REFERENCES

Aronson, Elliot. *The Social Animal*. New York: Worth Publishers, 1998.

Ashkenas, Ronald N., Lawrence J. DeMonaco, and Suzanne C. Francis. "Making the Deal Real: How GE Capital Integrates Acquisitions." *Harvard Business Review*, January–February 1998.

Baldock, Robert. *Destination Z: The History of the Future*. New York: John Wiley & Sons, Inc., 1998.

Barker, Joel Arthur. *Paradigms: The Business of Discovering the Future*. New York: Harper Business, 1993.

Berlyne, David E. "A Theory of Human Curiosity." *British Journal of Psychology*, 45 (1954): 180–191. Quoted in Hunt, Morton, *The Story of Psychology*. New York: Anchor Books, 1994.

Bridges, William. *Transitions: Making Sense of Life's Changes*. Reading, Massachusetts: Perseus Books, 1980.

Brodsky, Norm. "Hurry Up and Wait." *Inc.*, November 1998.

Byrne, John A. "The 21st Century Corporation: The Great Transformation." *Business Week*, August 28, 2000.

Carr, Nicholas G. "On the Edge: An Interview with George Conrades." *Harvard Business Review*, May–June 2000.

Cerf, Christopher, and Victor Navasky. *The Experts Speak: The Definitive Compendium of Authoritative Misinformation*. New York: Pantheon Books, 1984.

Charan, Ram, and Geoffrey Colvin. "Why CEOs Fail." *Fortune*, June 21, 1999.

Cialdini, Robert B. *Influence: The Psychology of Persuasion*. New York: William Morrow and Company, Inc., 1993.

Collins, James C., and Jerry I. Porras. *Built to Last: Successful Habits of Visionary Companies*. New York: HarperCollins Publishers, Inc., 1994.

Colvin, Geoffrey. "The Most Valuable Quality in a Manager." *Fortune*, December 29, 1997.

Cringely, Robert X. "The Best CEOs." *Worth*, May 1999.

Damasio, Antonio R., and Hanna Damasio. "Brain and Language." *Scientific American*, September 1992.

Fishman, Charles. "Face Time with Meg Whitman." *Fast Company*, May 2001.

Fishman, Charles. "Change." *Fast Company*, April 1997.

Frankl, Victor. *Man's Search for Meaning*. New York: Washington Square Press, 1985.

Freiberg, Kevin, and Jackie Freiberg. *Nuts! Southwest Airlines' Crazy Recipe for Business and Personal Success*. New York: Bantam Doubleday Dell, 1998.

Goleman, Daniel. *Vital Lies, Simple Truths: The Psychology of Self-Deception*. New York: A Touchstone Book, Published by Simon & Schuster, 1986.

Greenberg, Alan C. *Memos from the Chairman*. New York: Workman Publishing, 1996.

Grove, Andrew. *Only the Paranoid Survive: How to Exploit the Crisis Points That Challenge Every Company and Career*. New York: Currency Doubleday, 1996.

Hopkins, Tom. *How to Master the Art of Selling*. New York: Warner Books, Inc., 1982.

Hunt, Morton. *The Story of Psychology*. New York: Anchor Books, 1994.

Janis, Irving. *Victims of Groupthink: A Psychological Study of Foreign Decisions and Fiascos*. Boston: Houghton Mifflin, 1967.

James, Jennifer. *Thinking in the Future Tense*. New York: Simon & Schuster, 1996.

Kelly, Kevin. "The Roaring Zeros." *Wired*, September 1999.

Kelly, Kevin. *New Rules for the New Economy*. New York: Viking Penguin, 1998.

Kelly, Patrick. *Faster Company: Building the World's Nuttiest, Turn-on-a-Dime, Home-Grown, Billion-Dollar Business*. New York: John Wiley & Sons, Inc., 1998.

Kriegel, Robert, and David Brandt. *Sacred Cows Make the Best Burgers*. New York: Warner Books, 1996.

Marks, Robert. "Are You Next?" *Business 2.0*, March 1999.

Morris, William. *The American Heritage Dictionary*. Boston: Houghton Mifflin Company, 1985.

Neff, Thomas J., and James M. Citrin. *Lessons from the Top: The Search for America's Best Business Leaders.* New York: Currency Double-day, 1999.

Ordonez, Jennifer. "Burger King's Decision to Develop French Fry Has Been a Whopper." *The Wall Street Journal*, January 16, 2001.

O'Toole, James. *Leading Change: Overcoming the Ideology of Comfort and the Tyranny of Custom.* San Francisco: Jossey-Bass Publishers, 1995.

Peterson, Andrea. "Motorola Goes Into Mea Culpa Mode to Atone for Its Cellphone Blunders." *The Wall Street Journal*, May 18, 2001.

Pfeffer, Jeffrey. "The Real Keys to High Performance." *Leader to Leader*, Spring 1998.

Pinker, Steven. *How the Mind Works.* New York: W. W. Norton & Company, Inc., 1999.

Ransdell, Eric. "IBM's Grassroots Revival." *Fast Company*, October 1997.

Ratey, John. *A User's Guide to the Brain: Perception, Attention, and the Four Theaters of the Brain.* New York: Pantheon Books, 2001.

Rebello, Kathy. "Inside Microsoft: The Untold Story of How the Internet Forced Bill Gates to Reverse Course." *Business Week*, July 15, 1996.

Reber, Arthur. *Penguin Dictionary of Psychology.* Harmondsworth, Middlesex, England: Penguin Books Ltd., 1995.

Rozanski, Horacio, Gerry Bollman, and Martin Lipman. "Seize the Occasion." E-Insights: The Digital Customer Project. Booz-Allen & Hamilton, March 2001. Available at www.strategy-business.com.

Sager, Ira, and Diane Brady. "Big Blue's Blunt Bohemian." *Business Week*, June 14, 1999.

Schein, Edgar. "How Can Organizations Learn Faster? The Challenge of Entering the Green Room." *Sloan Management Review*, Winter 1993.

Schwartz, Peter. *The Art of the Long View: Planning for the Future in an Uncertain World.* New York: Currency Doubleday, 1996.

Senge, Peter. *The Fifth Discipline: The Art & Practice of the Learning Organization.* New York: Currency Doubleday, 1994.

Slywotzky, Adrian J., and David J. Morrison. *How Digital Is Your Business?* New York: Crown Business, 2000.

Stewart, Thomas. "A New Way to Think About Employees." *Fortune*, April 13, 1998.

Taylor, Alex III. "The Gentlemen at Ford Are Kicking Butt." *Fortune*, June 22, 1998.

Taylor, William C. "Whatever Happened to Globalization?" *Fast Company*, September 1999.

Thaye, Leah, ed. *Trend Letter*. The Global Business Network, January 21, 1999.

Weathersby, George B. "No Business Like e-Business." *Management Review*, November 1999.

Wetlaufer, Suzy. "From the Editors: For Crying Out Loud, Which Is It?" *Harvard Business Review*, May–June 2000.

ACKNOWLEDGMENTS

A book like this one isn't born without the assistance and influence of many, many people, so I take this opportunity to officially say thank you.

A giant thank you to my agent, Marta Justak, of Justak Literary Services, for her guidance, enthusiasm, and encouragement. I am very lucky to have Marta in my corner.

My gratitude to Airie Dekidjiev and Jessica Noyes of John Wiley & Sons, for their enthusiasm, suggestions, and editorial direction.

A special thank you to my mentor, former boss, and unofficial editor, Margie Cooke, for her patient review and excellent suggestions on my drafts of the proposal and of the manuscript. The thinking that led to this book was greatly influenced by the experience of working for Margie. Her picture should be in the dictionary next to the word *leader*.

To my friends, clients, and colleagues who took time out from their hectic businesses to listen, read, and offer encouragement and feedback on the book, thank you: Matt Arata, Gene Bennett, Tracey Haun, Gail Moncla, and John VanVliet. A very special thank you to Audrey Phillips, a talented artist and graphic designer, for her constant encouragement and insightful suggestions. This book would not have been born without Audrey.

A very special thank you to my cohorts, Dale Darling and Molly Machamer, for being the talented, flexible, inspirations that you are.

A special thank you to Linda Greck of MediaMatters, the best media pitcher I've ever met.

Thank you to Sandy Canfield and Dr. Mark Koltko-Rivera for their assistance in identifying psychological research.

To my current and former clients (and those who have attended seminars), who willingly experimented with my unorthodox ideas, provided feedback, and encouraged me to write this book, Thank You. Special thanks to: Jim Borel, Jane Brooks, Jim Collins, Katie Hewlett, Georgia Landrum, Gil Meyer, Carol McCaffrey, Doug Nail, Frank Owen, and Yale Schalk at DuPont; Tony Katz, Maryellen Nugent Lee, Layne Maly, Justin Shaw, Laura Sturtz, and Mark Weiss at The Rowland Company; Sharon Berry, Lou Calatayud, Alex Cellar, Ron Day, Bob Dickey, Paul Dechen and the PTI team, Dwain DeVille, Donna Dowless, Kevin Engel, Brett Fadeley, Doug Foreman, Rich Gibson, Carlos and Denise Giraldo and the Central Reservation Service team, Ben Grocock, Roger Hadley, Cindy Hasenau, Ken Hobbie, Susan Kendrick, Danny Klinefelter, Lorraine Lax, Chris Luelf, Ron Lukowski, Robin McCullough, Phil McLain, Susie Moore, Sharon Olsen, Jean Otte, Richard Owen, Ben Pittman, Ron Robbins, Jackie Rock, Wendy Sarcinella, Tom Shipley and the tshipley.com team, Janice Simcoe, Charlie Smith, Judy Stead, Renee Tanner, Leslie Temmen, Valerie Thompson, Sylvia Walters, Melanie Wegner, and Terry Wolf. A very special thank you to talented singer and songwriter Ruth King, who is a great client, cheerleader, and inspiration.

Thank you to my current and former colleagues. I have learned from you all. Thank you to my former colleagues at Saatchi & Saatchi, especially Katherine Childress, Dawn Harr, Ann Hayden, Chris Meyer, Craig Wood, and the members of the Saatchi Whack Attack team. Thank you to: Walt Albro, Steve Bedwell, Dave Bell, Caroline Breuche, Ray Casas, Mike Dooley, Nancy Forbes, Frank Fuerst, Stan Gross, Paul Kindinger, Scott Levitt, Diane Parnell, Bill Schuette, Marianne Shane, Tom Slabe, Karen Wenk, and Otis and Joanna Wragg.

A very special thank you to the "Motley Crew": Jerry Dunn, Alice Hannula, Jackie Hoxie, Mavis Kelley, Gail Kuhnlein, Jeanne Lipe, Julie Phelps, Martha Slater, and Willie Vinson. A special thank you also to Kenn Christopher, who encouraged me to explore the possibilities.

I am fortunate to be supported by a group of talented friends, who inspire and encourage me: Lisa and Bob Bowman, Traci Friess Clark, Andrea Hessinger, Mary Jacobson, Joyce, Steve, Jessica and Monica McCarthy, Jim Stiles, Sherri Sullivan, and Sheila Truman. Thank you.

To my wonderful family, who always support me, but especially for their help, suggestions, and encouragement during the writing process: Meri Bradford and Dave Hayes, Bill Bradford and Gloria Hecht, Shaunna, Mike, Eric, and Justin Wojtkowiak, Martha and Bill

Marshall, Dave and Sarah Marshall, Kelly and Eric Reeve, George and Sally Perles, Kathy Perles, Terry and Tracy Perles, John and Amy Perles, Pat and Karen Perles, and Jackie Davis. Thank you.

A big thank you to my "office staff," Anna Ruffcitti and Renata Gwiazda, and the team at the Altamonte Mail Boxes Etc., who go out of their way to make my life easier.

Special thanks to my coaches, Rosemary Taylor and Mary Connolly, for their insights and counsel.

To the many writers and speakers who have influenced and taught me, I would like to acknowledge my debt of gratitude for their wisdom, especially: Joel Barker, Warren Bennis, Roger Blackwell, William Bridges, John Seely Brown, Tony Buzan, John Byrne, Jim Collins, Thomas Davenport, Elaine de Beauport, Peter Drucker, Wayne Dyer, Michael Gelb, Seth Godin, Gary Hamel, Charles Handy, Jean Houston, Jennifer James, Kevin Kelly, Caroline Myss, Tom Peters, Thomas Petzinger, Jr., Peter Schwartz, Peter Senge, Patricia Seybold, Thomas Stewart, Jim Taylor, William Taylor, Watts Wacker, Denis Waitley, and Alan Webber.

My heartfelt gratitude to each and every one of you.

Shannon Bradford

ABOUT THE AUTHOR

Shannon Bradford is a popular business speaker, trainer, and coach. She is the CEO and Chief Thinkologist of Mind Capital, and specializes in helping business people think more powerfully, innovate, work together effectively, and succeed in the new, brain-based business world. Their clients include individuals and teams from a wide range of organizations—from small technology companies to not-for-profit associations to government to global Fortune 500 companies.

Shannon holds a master's degree in human communication from Michigan State University. Her professional experience is in small business, government, and most recently, the business-to-business group of Saatchi & Saatchi, a global advertising agency.

Shannon's services include speeches, workshops, seminars, retreats, and individual and team coaching. For more information about Shannon's speaking, training, or coaching services, or to sign up for her e-mail newsletter, click on www.mindcapital.com, or call 1-800-732-6789.

INDEX